Oxford Picture Dictionary of American English

WORKBOOK

Oxford Picture Dictionary of American English
WORKBOOK

Jill Wagner Schimpff

New York Oxford
OXFORD UNIVERSITY PRESS
1981

Oxford University Press

200 Madison Avenue, New York, N.Y. 10016 USA

Walton Street, Oxford OX2 6DP England

OXFORD is a trademark of Oxford University Press, Inc.

ISBN 0-19-502819-8

Design and illustrations: Elizabeth Baecher.

Printing (last digit): 10 9

Printed in the United States of America.

To my husband, Warren, who had to figure out all the puzzles and play all the games!

Contents

To the Teacher

This **Workbook** has been specifically designed to accompany the *Oxford Picture Dictionary of American English*. It is suitable for students at the junior high school through adult level using any of the four editions of the *Oxford Picture Dictionary*.

The main purpose of the **Workbook** is to provide practice with and reinforcement of the vocabulary presented in the *Oxford Picture Dictionary* through exercises and activities. The exercises are not necessarily intended to be covered in sequence since it is assumed that most teachers do not proceed through the *Picture Dictionary* in consecutive order, from cover to cover. Page numbers inside the symbol

preceding each exercise, refer to the page of the *Picture Dictionary* which is correlated with that exercise. Naturally, the teacher must introduce and clarify the vocabularv before related **Workbook** pages are attempted.

It is hoped that a variety of uses can be made of individual exercises. For example, although a fill-in-the-blank exercise may stress vocabulary retention, it may also be a good reading exercise or a lesson on the use of articles. Many of the exercises throughout the **Workbook** are particularly valuable for stimulating discussion. Each exercise has been marked for level of difficulty to aid teachers in selecting exercises to suit the particular needs of their students. One bullet ■ indicates an easy exercise, two bullets ■ ■, an exercise of average difficulty and three bullets ■ ■ ■ indicate a more challenging exercise. Throughout the **Workbook**, brown ink is used to indicate examples and sample answers. If a student, for example, is to locate and circle words in a puzzle, one of the words will be circled in brown to provide the model. This convention should be explained initially to the students and thereafter it should be evident to them.

The *Appendix* at the back of the **Workbook** includes basic information on numbers, time and dates, as well as the alphabet in block and cursive letters. Students, especially those unfamiliar with the Roman alphabet, may find this a useful tool. An *Answer Key* is also provided at the back of the **Workbook**.

The **Workbook** is the fourth component of our comprehensive vocabulary program. The other components include the four editions of the *Oxford Picture Dictionary*: Monolingual English, English-Spanish, English-Japanese, and French-Indexed; *Wall Charts* and a *Cassette Pack*.

Oxford Picture Dictionary of American English

WORKBOOK

4 Our Universe

■ Start in the center and go around the spinning galaxy to find eight of the twelve words below.

sun	**moon**	**nosecone**	**constellation**	**astronaut**
rocket	**satellite**	**eclipse**	**orbit**	**launch pad**
comet	**star**			

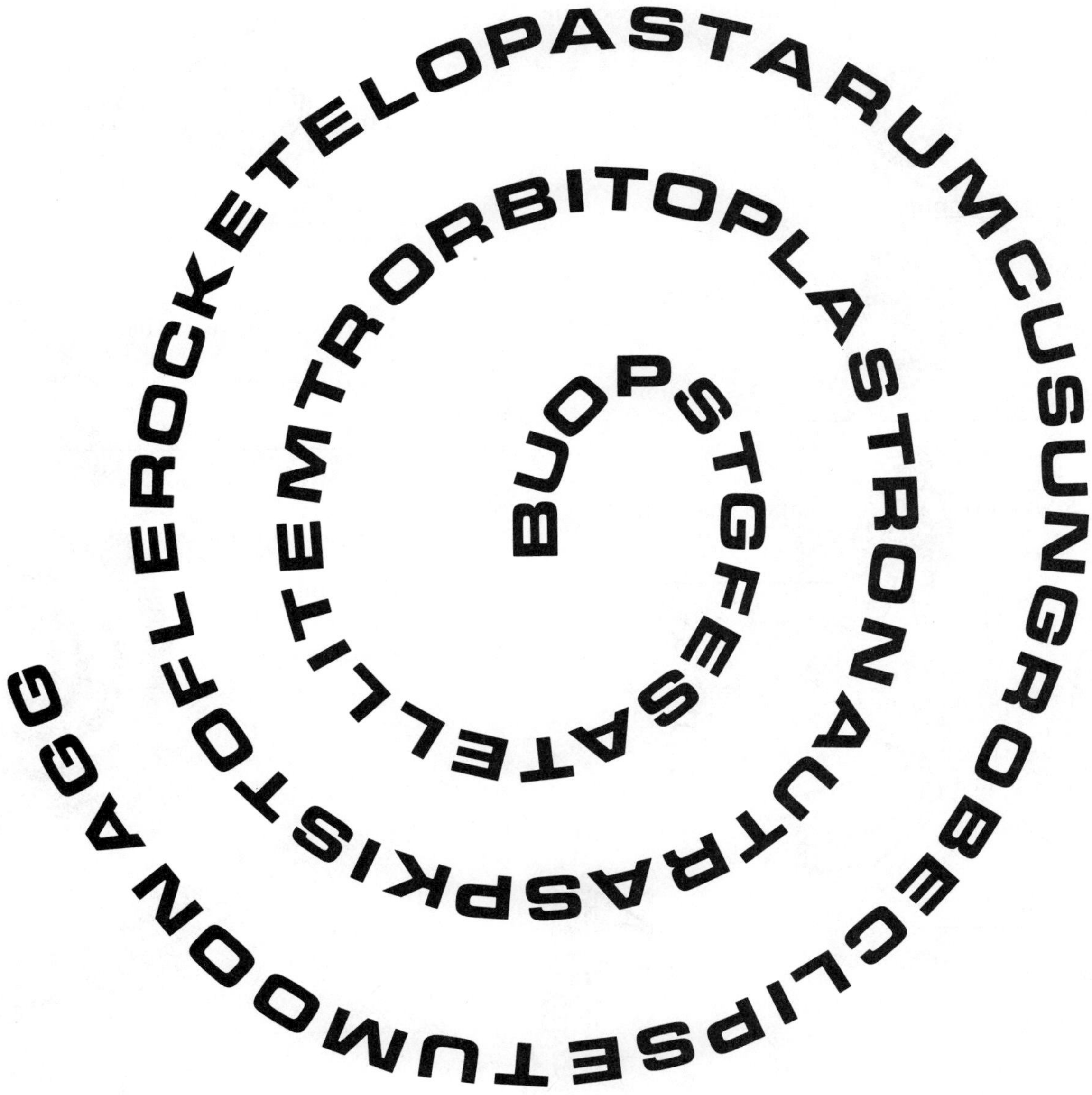

Using the first letter of each word you found, fill in the blanks below to find the answer to the puzzle.

PUZZLE: This is what we call the sun and all the planets that orbit the sun. _ _ l _ _ _ y _ t _ _

4 Our Universe

■ Look at the pictures and choose the correct answer from the following words. You will not use all of the words.

galaxy	**planet**	**space capsule**	**full moon**	**orbit**
comet	**earth**	**launching pad**	**spacesuit**	**space**
sun	**eclipse**	**astronaut**	**stars**	
constellation	**nosecone**			

1. The  is round.

   full moon

2. A (an)  is part of a rocket ship.

   ____

3. A (an)  wears a spacesuit.

   ____

4. A special group of  ______________

   is a (an) 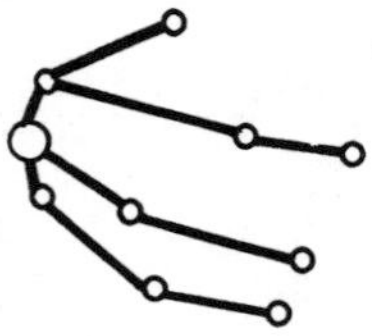

   ______________.

5. A rocket sits on a (an) 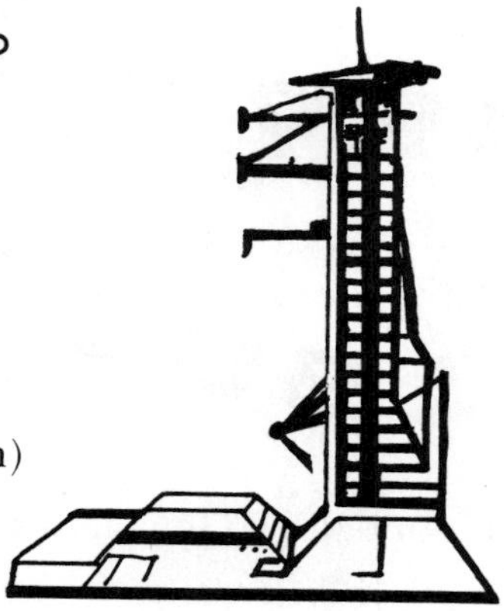

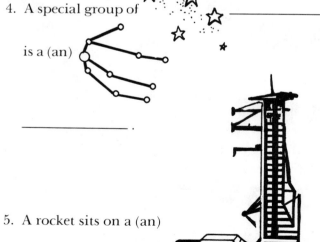

   ______________ ______________.

6. The  is a (an) 

   ______________ ______________.

7. An astronaut sits in the 

   of a rocket ship.

   ______________ ______________

8. Our planet is part of a very big 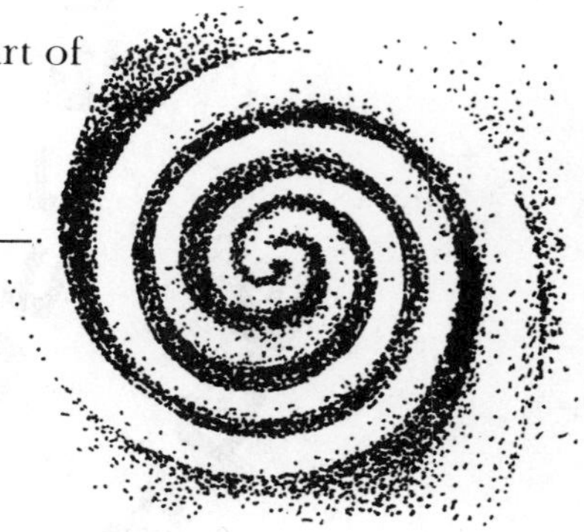

   ______________.

9. A (an) 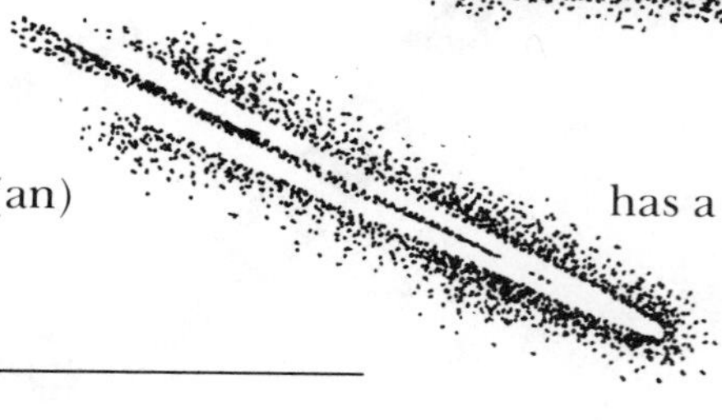 has a long tail.

   ____

10. The earth orbits the 

   ______________.

5-7 The World

Which word does **not** belong to the group? Underline the one which does **not** fit. Be ready to give reasons for your answers.

1. Andes Alps Ganges Urals It is not a mountain range.
2. Amazon Antarctic Asia Australia
3. lake island estuary bay
4. Danube Atlantic Indian Pacific
5. Arabian Kalahari Gobi Mekong
6. Nile Mississippi Congo Niger
7. North Sea Red Sea South China Sea Caspian Sea
8. Antarctic Circle Tropic of Capricorn Tropic of Cancer
9. line of longitude line of latitude coastline
10. Asia Africa Arctic Antarctica
11. Persian Gulf Gulf of Alaska Gulf of Mexico
12. North America Australia South America

5-7 The World

■ Read the following sentences. Underline the word that needs a capital letter. Put that word in the crossword puzzle below.

ACROSS

1. The arctic is colder than the oceans south of it.
2. The continent of australia is southeast of Asia.
3. My friend robert lives on a beautiful island.
4. The city of dacca is near a wide river delta.

DOWN

5. Our plane is flying over the indus, a very famous river.
6. Many boats sail on the gulf of Mexico.
7. The sahara is the largest desert in the world.
8. The South pole is far from any large lake.
9. Hudson bay looks larger than the sea I saw yesterday on the map.
10. It is easy to find the andes on a globe.

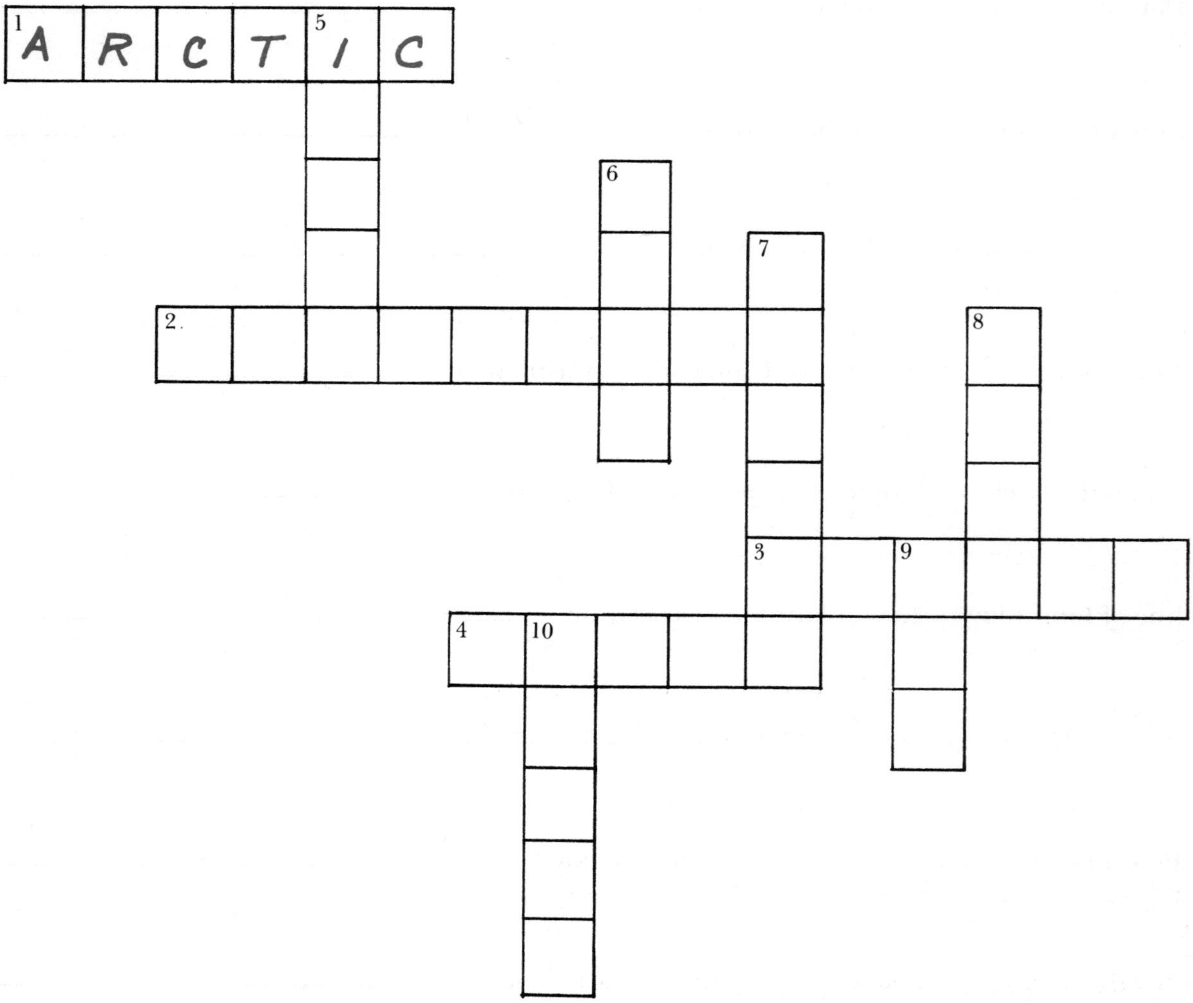
1 A R C T 5 I C
6
7
2.
8
3
9
4
10

5-7

The World

Use the following words to fill in the blanks below. You will not use all of the words.

Pacific	**Red**	**Europe**	**Danube**	**Baltic**
Black	**Asia**	**Gobi**	**Mekong**	**Congo**
Amazon	**Alps**	**Yellow**	**Hudson**	**Africa**
Andes	**Kalahari**	**Mediterranean**	**Tasman**	**Arabian**
Yangtze	**Alaska**	**North**	**Nile**	

1. The continent north of Africa is ____Europe____.

2. The ____________ Sea is southwest of the Persian Gulf.

3. The desert in the middle of Asia is the ____________ Desert.

4. The large bay in the northeast part of North America is the ____________ Bay.

5. The mountains running in a north-south direction on the west coast of South America are the ____________.

6. The river which runs in a north-south direction in Africa is the ____________.

7. The ____________ Sea is north of Africa.

8. The ____________ Sea is northeast of the Mediterranean Sea.

9. The continent which has a huge desert in the north is ____________.

10. The three rivers which almost meet in southeast Asia are the ____________ River, the ____________ River, and the ____________ River.

11. The desert in southwest Africa is the ____________.

12. The gulf in the northwest part of North America is the Gulf of ____________.

13. The mountains which run in an east-west direction in Europe are the ____________.

8 The Human Body

■ **A. The Skeleton** **B. The Body**

Match the following parts of the body with the place where they are found.

A. leg
B. arm
C. hand
D. foot
E. head

1. A	knee	7. ____	ankle
2. ____	palm	8. ____	thumb
3. ____	elbow	9. ____	calf
4. ____	finger	10. ____	hair
5. ____	instep	11. ____	fist
6. ____	thigh	12. ____	toe

■ Look at the pictures below and unscramble the letters.

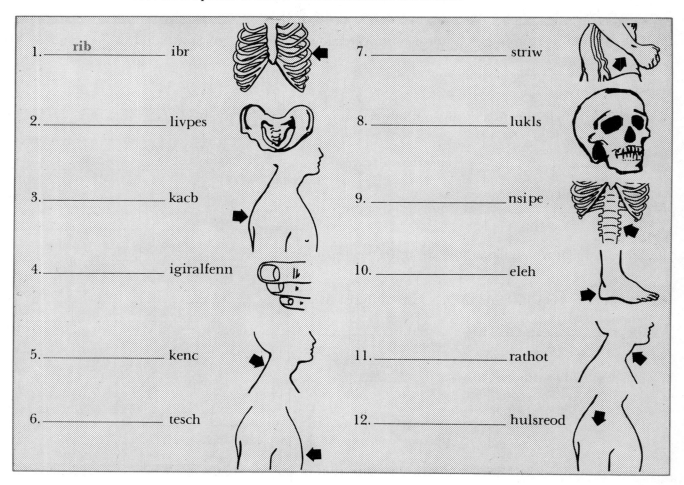

1. rib ibr
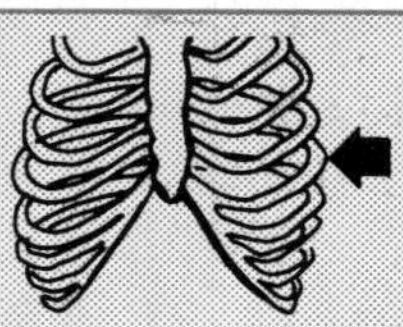

2. ____ livpes

3. ____ kacb
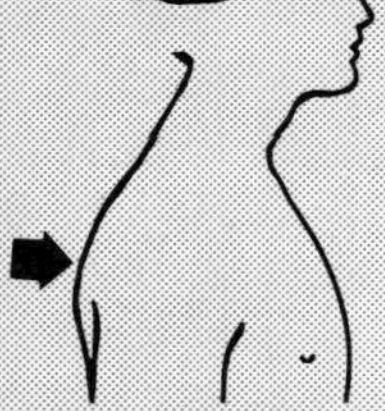

4. ____ igiralfenn

5. ____ kenc

6. ____ tesch
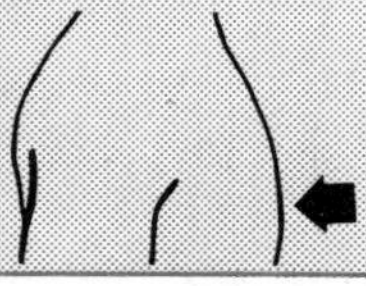

7. ____ striw

8. ____ lukls

9. ____ nsipe
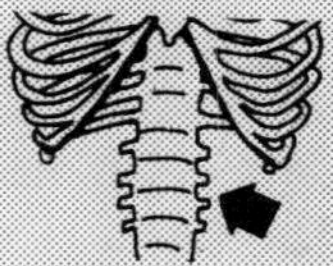

10. ____ eleh
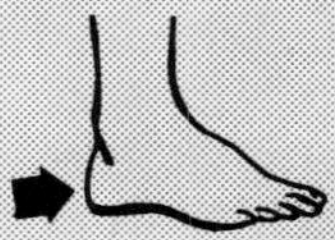

11. ____ rathot

12. ____ hulsreod
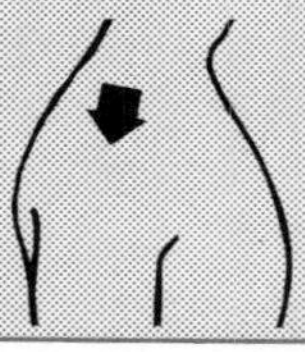

9 The Human Body

C. The Face **D. The Eye** **E. The Insides**

■ ■ Find the answers by using the following words. One of the words will not be used.

vein	**nose**	**temple**	**muscle**	**mustache**
heart	**windpipe**	**mouth**	**brain**	**lung**
eyebrow	**cheek**	**pupil**	**eyelashes**	**kidney**
iris	**beard**	**tongue**	**tooth**	
chin		**artery**		

1. Used for eating: **mouth**
2. Over the eye: ____________
3. To the side of the mouth: ____________
4. An opening in the eye: ____________
5. Used to smell: ____________
6. Sends blood to all parts of the body: ____________
7. Used for hard work: ____________
8. Hair along the jaw: ____________
9. Hard, white, and in the mouth: ____________
10. Used to think: ____________
11. Under the mouth: ____________
12. Hairs on the eyelids: ____________
13. Hair over the top lip: ____________
14. The colored part of the eye: ____________
15. Carries blood to the heart: ____________
16. Used to talk: ____________
17. Between the eye and the ear: ____________
18. It's part of the chest and is used to breathe: ____________
19. Carries air from the mouth to the lungs: ____________
20. Carries blood from the heart: ____________

10 Clothes: Men and Boys

■ Look at the picture in your *Oxford Picture Dictionary* and correct these sentences.

1. The boy on the left is wearing a jacket. — **No, the boy on the left is wearing a bathrobe.**
2. The boy on the right has tennis shoes on. ______
3. The boy in the middle has jeans on. ______
4. There is a pair of slippers in the middle of the room. ______
5. The boy on the right is wearing a sport coat. ______
6. The boy on the left is wearing slacks. ______
7. The boy in the middle is wearing a sweater. ______
8. The boy in the middle is not wearing socks. — **No, the boy in the middle is wearing socks.**
9. The boy on the right is not wearing a belt. ______
10. The boy on the left is wearing socks. ______

11 Clothes: Men and Boys

■ Use the following words to fill in the blanks below. You will not use all of the words.

cuff	**briefcase**	**collar**	**lapel**	**button**
pocket	**slacks**	**watch**	**raincoat**	**shoelace**
sole	**gloves**	**scarf**	**overcoat**	**glasses**

1. What time is it? I need a new ________________.
2. It is very cold today and my jacket is not warm enough. Where is my ________________?
3. Put your money in your ________________.
4. It looks like rain. Put on your ________________.
5. I need to take some papers to the office. Where is my ________________?
6. My shoe is so old that there's a hole in the ________________.
7. My hands are cold. Where are my ________________?
8. Wash your shirt! The cuffs and ________________ are dirty.
9. My eyes are not very good. I need ________________.
10. These ________________ don't go with my green sport coat.
11. I have a sore throat and must keep warm. Where is my ________________?
12. I lost a ________________ from my new shirt.
13. She pinned a flower to the ________________ of my suit jacket.

■ Combine the following words to make new words. Then write these words below.

brief	
over	band
shoe	lace
watch	coat
trench	case
rain — (coat)	

________________ ________________ ________________

________________ ________________ ________________

8, 9, 12

Clothes: Women and Girls

■ Match the article on the left with the part of the body on which it is used.

1.	G	nail polish	**A.**	**hair**
2.	______	ring	**B.**	**eyelashes**
3.	______	slipper	**C.**	**eyelid**
4.	______	brush	**D.**	**wrist**
5.	______	earring	**E.**	**neck**
6.	______	mascara	**F.**	**lips**
7.	______	eye shadow	**G.**	**fingernails**
8.	______	bracelet	**H.**	**foot**
9.	______	necklace	**I.**	**ear**
10.	______	lipstick	**J.**	**finger**

■ ■ Look at the picture on page 13 in your *Oxford Picture Dictionary* and complete the following description.

Two mothers and their daughters are walking in the park. The lady on the left is wearing a white ______________ and a purple ______________. She is carrying a brown ______________. Her friend is wearing a red ______________ and a red and gray ______________. She is holding a white ______________.

Their daughters are talking. The girl on the left is wearing a brown ______________ and a brown and white ______________. She is also wearing white ______________. Her friend is wearing a brown ______________ over a red and white ______________. She is also wearing blue ______________. She has brown ______________ on her feet. They are having a good time.

10-13 Clothes

■ Put the following words into the correct categories below. Two of the words fit into two categories.

boots	**panties**	**loafers**	**shorts**	**nightgown**
bathrobe	**bracelet**	**lipstick**	**sneakers**	**umbrella**
mascara	**eye shadow**	**T-shirt**	**bra**	**slip**
cuff links	**rain hat**	**trenchcoat**	**rubber boots**	**ring**
socks	**panty hose**	**pajamas**	**necklace**	**nail polish**
slippers	**earrings**			

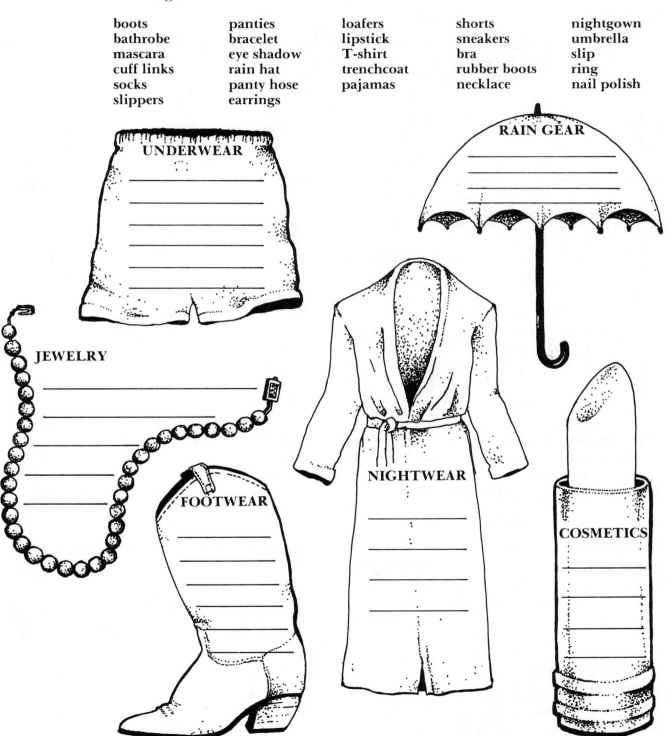

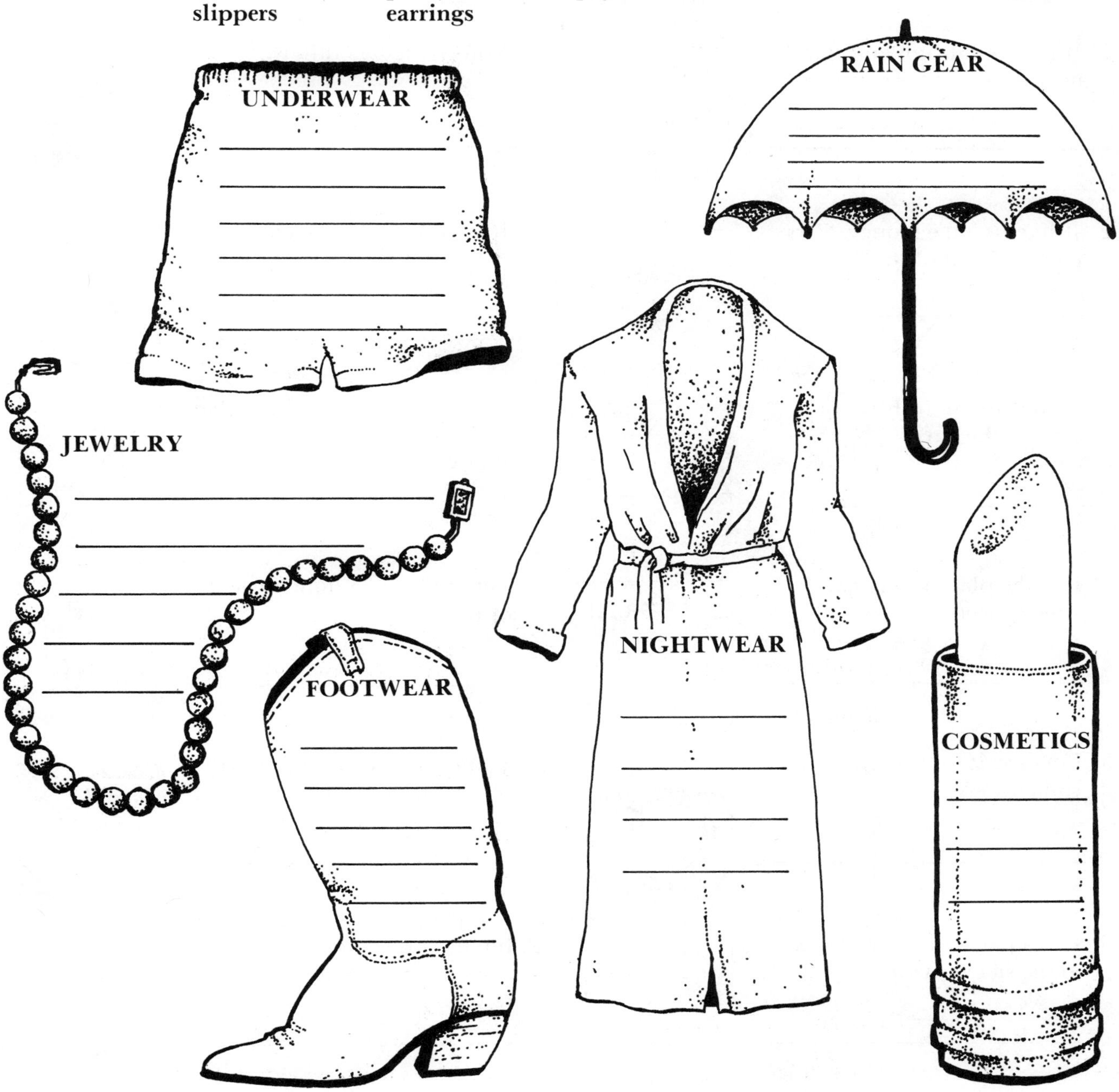
UNDERWEAR
RAIN GEAR
JEWELRY
NIGHTWEAR
FOOTWEAR
COSMETICS

14-15

In the City

■ Choose from the following words to answer each puzzle. You will not use all of the words.

street light	**crosswalk**	**gutter**	**drain**	**bus stop**
parking lot	**sidewalk**	**baby carriage**	**trash can**	**display window**
parking meter	**bridge**	**subway station**	**intersection**	**mailbox**
traffic light	**van**	**telephone booth**		

1. It is a round sign and stands near the corner of the street.

____

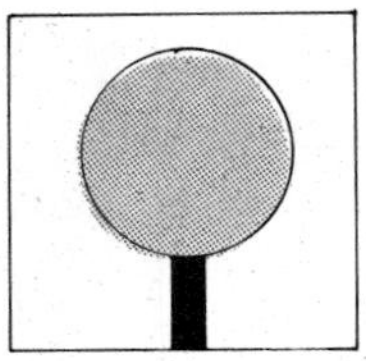

2. It likes to take money. Cars park in front of it.

____

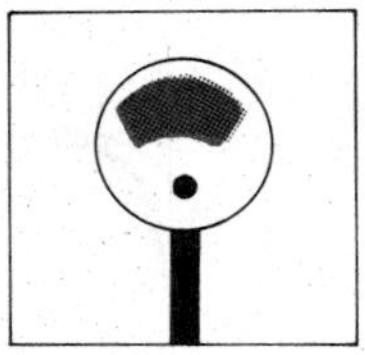

3. You walk on it. It is not a part of the street.

____

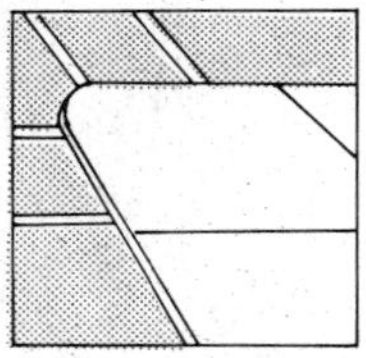

4. It is the place where two streets meet.

____

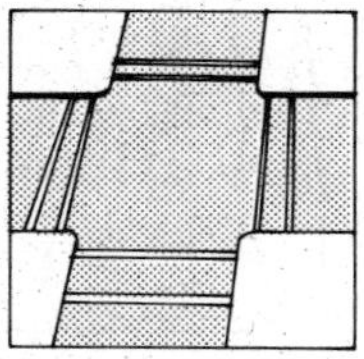

5. Cars use it to travel over something.

____

6. It is a part of the street next to the sidewalk.

____

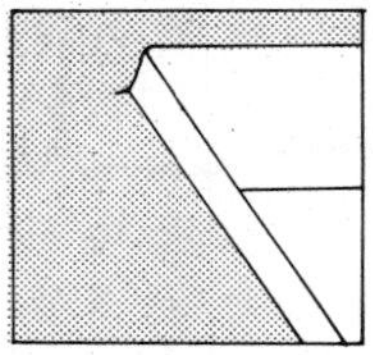

7. You put letters into it.

____

8. It is not as large as a bus or truck, but it is larger than a car.

____

9. They are two white lines that go from one street corner to another.

____

10. You find a telephone inside of it.

____

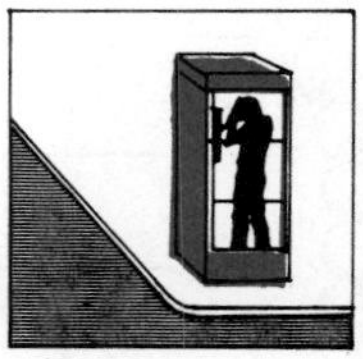

11. You can look through it to see things for sale.

____

12. It tells you to stop or go.

____

14–15

In the City

■ ■ Which word does **not** belong to the group? Underline the one which does **not** fit. Be ready to give reasons for your answers.

There is more than one possible answer for some of the puzzles.

1. bus taxi truck **It does not carry passengers.**
2. van motorcycle bicycle ____
3. office building apartment house parking lot ____
4. mailbox bus stop trash can ____
5. sidewalk bridge street ____
6. sewer subway station mailbox ____
7. crosswalk park intersection ____
8. traffic light street sign bus stop ____
9. motorcycle baby carriage truck ____
10. bus stop street sign trash can ____

■ ■ ■ On the lines below describe the city or town where *you* live. Use as much of the vocabulary from *In the City* as possible.

____

____

____

____

____

16 The Law

■ ■ Are you a good policeman? Can you discover what this says? Look at the key at the bottom of the page. As you read the story, put in the correct letter for each number to find out what happens.

THE ROBBERY

It is late at night and Officer Jones, a ____________________, is using his ____________________ to see
16-15-12-9-3-5-13-1-14 6-12-1-19-8-12-9-7-8-20

the inside of a jewelry store. His dark ________________ makes it difficult to see him. He and his police
21-14-9-6-15-18-13

______ walk down the street to call the police ________________. In a few minutes a police ______
4-15-7 19-20-1-20-9-15-14 3-1-18

meets the policeman in front of the store. Three policemen enter the store through an open window.

One of them stands __________ at the back door with a ____________________ in his hand. The other
7-21-1-18-4 14-9-7-8-20-19-20-9-3-11

two search for __________________________ with a ___________________ ____________. "This looks
6-9-14-7-5-18-16-18-9-14-20-19 13-1-7-14-9-6-25-9-14-7 7-12-1-19-19

like the work of Fast ______ Pete," said one officer. "In a case last year a __________ and __________ let
7-21-14 10-21-4-7-5 10-21-18-25

him go because we had no ________________ to put on the witness __________ and no other evidence.
23-9-20-14-5-19-19 19-20-1-14-4

He had a good _____________ ___________________. This time, if we find fingerprints, we will soon
4-5-6-5-14-19-5 1-20-20-15-18-14-5-25

have him in a _________ and behind _________!"
3-5-12-12 2-1-18-19

Key:

A	B	C	D	E	F	G	H	I	J	K	L	M	N	O
1	2	3	4	5	6	7	8	9	10	11	12	13	14	15

P	Q	R	S	T	U	V	W	X	Y	Z
16	17	18	19	20	21	22	23	24	25	26

17 Fire and Medical Services

■ Read the following sentences. Underline the word that is misspelled in each sentence. Correct the spelling and write the correctly spelled word in the crossword puzzle below.

ACROSS

1. The dentist moved the lamp and the dril a little closer to the patient.
2. The dentest said hello to his patient.
3. The pateint took off his bandage.
4. The doctor with the stethoscope used the fire extinwisher to put out the fire.
5. The nurse put his bandeege on in the hospital.
6. The fireman looked for his poot when he heard the bell ring.
7. They took the injured fireman to the nearest hosbital.
8. We could see smoak coming from the window by the fire escape.
9. The hoze will not reach the building that is on fire.

DOWN

1. The fire debartment has many assistants.
2. The patient liked his doctore very much.
3. The dental asistant made a trip to the hospital.
4. The nurse called for a fire engin.
5. The fireman picked up the nozle and ran towards the smoke.
6. The nerse put the sling on carefully.
7. The patient walked out of the hospital on clutches.
8. The fireman is standing by the fire hydrent.
9. The fireman climbed the latter with the nozzle in his hand.

DRILL

18 Education: In School

■ ■ All of the following scrambled words have something to do with the classroom. Can you figure them out? Use the clues to help you unscramble the words.

1. hlack	Students write on the board with it.	chalk
2. racledan	It tells you the date.	______
3. erlur	It measures the length of things.	______
4. scapmos	It makes a circle.	______
5. amp	It tells you where you are.	______
6. luge	It sticks things together.	______
7. torpcatorr	It measures the degrees of a circle.	______
8. dlise lure	It answers math questions quickly.	______
9. ralcabokbd	It is usually in the front of the classroom.	______
10. heceatr	This person helps students.	______
11. enp	It uses ink.	______
12. sked	A student sits at it.	______
13. neclip	You use it to write with.	______
14. nustted	This person learns a lot.	______
15. rersea	It removes writing.	______

19 Education: In the Science Laboratory

■ Circle the word that completes the sentence correctly. Then write the word in the crossword puzzle below.

ACROSS

1. You find a pan on a (scale, bench).
2. You use a (tripod, weight) with a Bunsen burner.
3. You use a (burner, pestle) with a mortar.
4. You find a pointer on a (lens, dial).
5. You find a (needle, tripod) on a dial.

DOWN

1. You use a (slide, flask) with a microscope.
2. You use rubber (meters, tubing) with a Bunsen burner.
3. A (pipette, crystal) is used with a flask or beaker.
4. A (magnet, beaker) is a glass container.
5. A (lens, dial) is part of a microscope.

SCALE

20 In the Supermarket

■ Fill in the blanks below by using the following words. Then, find the words in the puzzle at the bottom of the page. Some go across and others go down.

cheese	**sack**	**clerk**	**canned**	**shelf**
eggs	**vegetables**	**freezer**	**milk**	**cashier**
fruit	**bills**	**receipt**	**bread**	

ACROSS

1. Oranges, apples, and grapes are fruit.
2. Beans, peas, and potatoes are ____________.
3. Another word for bag is ____________.
4. Chickens lay ____________.
5. You can find ice cream in the ____________.
6. Cows produce ____________.
7. You can find canned food on the ____________.

DOWN

1. A cashier is the person who takes your money.
2. ____________ is often yellow and is a milk product.
3. Food that comes in a can is called ____________ food.
4. ____________ are paper money.
5. A ____________ is a person who can help you find things in the supermarket.
6. A ____________ is a long piece of paper with numbers on it.
7. Use two pieces of ____________ to make a sandwich.

E	B	R	O	T	S	E	H	T	O	T	O	G	B	T	N	A	C	I
F	R	E	E	Z	E	R	Y	S	S	E	L	N	I	E	G	G	S	U
H	E	T	H	S	C	A	C	E	M	O	S	E	L	M	E	V	I	G
T	A	M	O	R	H	F	R	T	X	G	W	A	L	C	I	T	A	C
E	D	D	R	V	E	G	E	T	A	B	L	E	S	I	A	H	H	A
F	T	N	A	C	E	S	C	T	O	R	A	P	M	R	E	C	S	N
O	C	S	A	L	S	E	E	M	I	L	K	W	S	A	Y	A	L	N
G	S	C	K	N	E	A	I	H	T	S	O	O	T	A	K	S	C	E
F	R	L	E	D	N	O	P	W	A	S	I	G	N	I	V	H	I	D
X	R	E	E	Y	F	O	T	E	M	I	T	L	F	R	U	I	T	U
T	E	R	S	S	A	C	K	T	N	I	O	P	T	I	Z	E	A	M
A	C	K	E	B	S	E	L	A	H	W	E	V	A	S	A	R	I	T
C	N	U	R	C	Z	A	G	S	H	E	L	F	E	H	T	E	S	N

20 In the Supermarket

■ ■ You are going food shopping. Make your own shopping list. Buy enough food for four days—breakfasts, lunches, and dinners.

BREAKFASTS	LUNCHES	DINNERS
1 dozen eggs	1 package of hot dogs	1 lb. of fish

■ ■ ■ Describe your favorite dish. Tell what ingredients go into it and how to prepare it.

Name of Dish: ______________________

Ingredients: ______________________

____

____

Recipe: ______________________

____

____

____

____

21 In the Office

■ Look at the picture for each sentence and then write the missing word in the crossword puzzle below.

ACROSS

1. A  helps answer math problems.

2. A 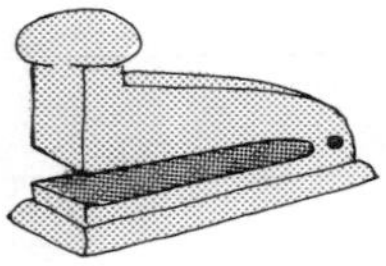 keeps papers together.

3. A 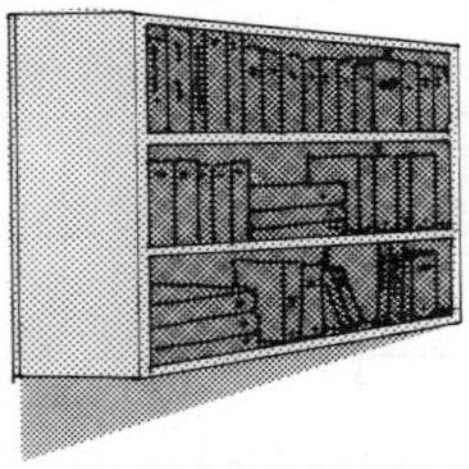 is a good place to find a dictionary.

4. A  absorbs ink.

5. A 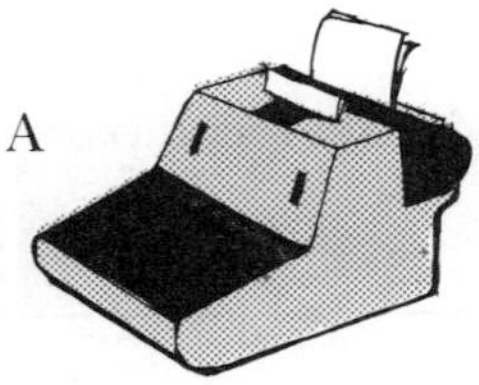 helps you to write fast.

DOWN

1. A  tells you the date.

7. A stenographer uses a 

DOWN

8. A 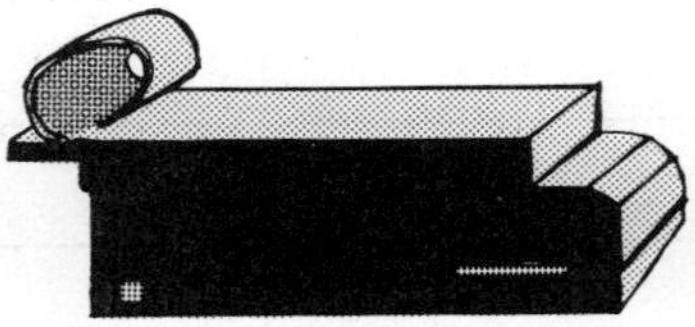 helps you copy papers fast.

9. The 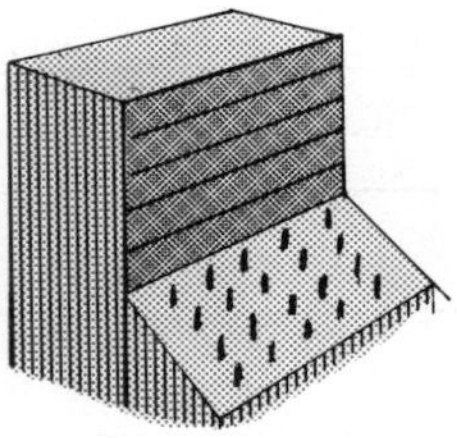 operator receives all telephone calls.

10. Put the papers into the 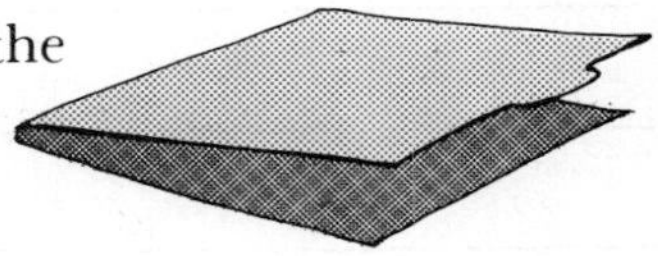

9
1 CALCULATOR
7
2
10
8
3
4
5

21 In the Office

Use the following words to fill in the blanks in the story below. Be careful of spelling! Not all of the words will be used.

office
desk
telephone
calculator
blotter
pencil holder
hole puncher
stapler
adding machine
paper clip
bulletin board
envelope
secretary
in-box
receptionist
photocopier
switchboard
operator
calendar
card file
file
file cabinet
carbon paper
typewriter
wastepaper basket
appointment book
steno pad
bookcase

A BUSY DAY!

The o f f i c e is a busy place. Yesterday it was very busy. Mrs. Johnson, the _ w _ _ c _ b _ _ r _   _ p _ r _ _ _ r, got many _ _ _ e p _ _ _ e calls. The _ _ c _ _ t _ _ n _ _ _ 's _ p _ _ i _ t _ _ n _ book was filled for the day. Many people came in to look at notices on the _ _ l _ e _ i _   _ o _ r _.

At 9:15 the _ h _ t _ _ _ p _ _ r broke down. At 9:30 the boss, Mr. Davis, complained because the _ _ c _ _ t _ _ y, Miss James, forgot to put c _ r _ o _   p _ _ e _ behind the sheets of paper in the t _ p _ w _ _ t _ _. Because the photocopier was broken, it was not possible to make more copies. After lunch, the mailman arrived and put thirty _ n v _ l _ _ e s in the _ n - b _ _. Miss James did not have time to read the letters. She worked all afternoon with the a _ d _ n _   _ a _ _ i _ e and the c _ l _ u _ a _ _ _.

When it was time to go home, Miss James could not find her keys. She looked everywhere around her _ e _ k. She looked under the _ l _ t _ e _, in the p _ _ c _ l   _ o _ _ e _, in the _ a _ d   _ i _ e, and in the w _ s _ e _ a _ _ r   _ _ s _ _ t. Finally she found them in the _ i l _   c _ b _ n _ t. She was glad that it was Friday!

22 At the Post Office

■ Make six new words by matching the following words. Draw a line between the words which go together.

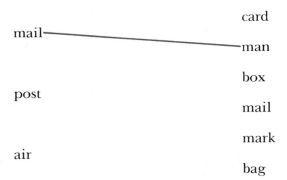

	card
mail —	— man
	box
post	mail
	mark
air	bag

■ ■ ■ Write sentences using the words below. Use some of the new words you found, too.

1. string package

____

____

2. stamp address

____

____

3. money order postal clerk

____

____

4. return address zip code

____

____

5. flap envelope

____

____

6. scale counter

____

____

22 At the Post Office

■ Address this envelope to a friend or relative in another country. Put your return address on the envelope and don't forget your zip code.

■ ■ ■ Write a postcard to a friend in the country in which you are now living. Tell your friend that you are learning English!

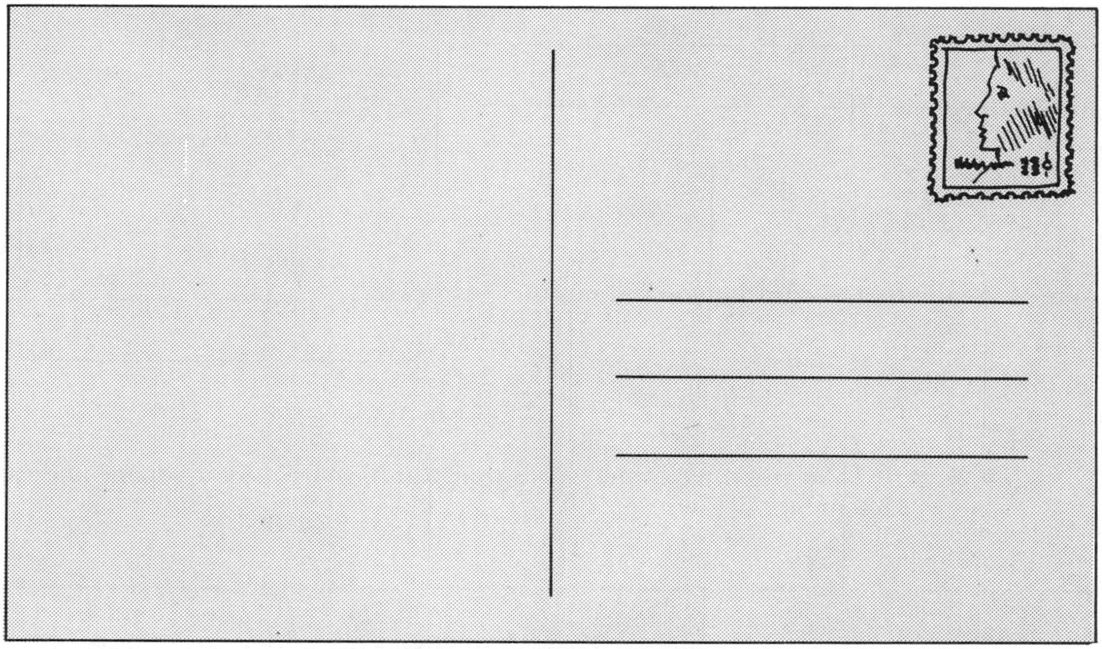

23 On a Building Site

■ Put the following words into the correct categories below. Two of the words will **not** fit into any category.

foundations	**excavator**	**wheelbarrow**	**shingle**	**shovel**
trowel	**hod**	**level**	**rafter**	**cement mixer**
scaffolding	**bricklayer**	**dump truck**	**workman**	**pick**

PEOPLE

____

____

LARGE MACHINERY

____

____

____

SMALL TOOLS

____

____

____

____

____

PARTS OF A BUILDING

____

____

____

Which are the two words that you did not use? ______________________

____

■ ■ ■ Take any three of the words that you have used on this page and use them in a sentence below.

____

____

23 On a Building Site

■ ■ Using twelve of the fourteen words below, fill in the blank spaces. The following clues and rhymes will help you. Then put the answers into the crossword puzzle.

workman	**brick**	**ladder**	**rafter**	**level**
crane	**board**	**sand**	**shingle**	**hod**
rung	**pick**	**trowel**	**cement**	

ACROSS

1. Made of wood and rhymes with Ford: board
2. A machine that lifts and rhymes with rain: ________________
3. Used to lay bricks and rhymes with rent: ________________
4. Used to cover a roof and rhymes with jingle: ________________
5. Used to carry cement and rhymes with rod: ________________

DOWN

4. Found at the beach and rhymes with land: ________________
6. Used to dig and rhymes with kick: ________________

DOWN

7. Part of a ladder and rhymes with tongue: ________________
8. Holds up the roof and rhymes with laughter: ________________
9. Used to spread cement and rhymes with growl: ________________
10. Each one helps build a house and rhymes with sick: ________________
11. Has a bubble in it and rhymes with devil: ________________

BOARD

24 In a Workshop

■ Check the correct box.

	Yes	No
1. The screwdriver is on the workbench.	☐	☒
2. The file is on the wall.	☐	☐
3. The powersaw is on the workbench.	☐	☐
4. The extension cord is on the shelf.	☐	☐
5. The axe is on the wall.	☐	☐

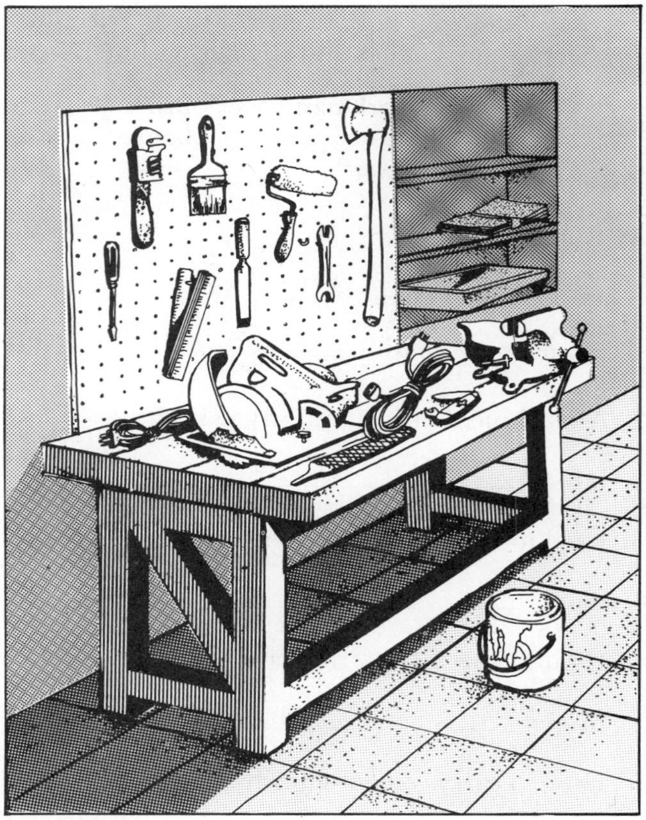

■ Now, write it out!

1. The vise is on the workbench. **Yes, it is.** ______
2. The chisel is on the shelf. **No, it isn't.** ______
3. The paint can is on the floor. ______
4. The paint pan is on the floor. ______
5. The pocket knife is on the workbench. ______

■ Now, correct the sentence!

1. The sandpaper is on the wall. **No, it isn't. It's on the shelf.** ______
2. The paintbrush is on the floor. ______
3. The monkey wrench is on the workbench. ______
4. The paint roller is on the shelf. ______

24 25

In a Workshop: Tools

■ ■ Which word does **not** belong to the group? Underline the one which does **not** fit. Be ready to give reasons for your answers.

1. pocket knife saw hacksaw <u>nail</u> **It doesn't cut.**
2. mallet pliers hammer ______
3. roller vise pan paintbrush ______
4. bolt nail screw ______
5. drill brace bit ______
6. sandpaper file shelf ______
7. axe hatchet plane ______
8. washer extension cord nut ______
9. handle hammer head ______
10. screwdriver workbench shelf ______

■ ■ You have a job to do. Which tools would you choose? You may have more than one answer.

1. Fix a leaky pipe. ______
2. Make a wooden table. ______
3. Paint a room. ______
4. Pull out some nails from a wall. ______

26 A House

■ Read the following sentences. Underline the word that is misspelled in each sentence. Then correct the spelling and write the word in the crossword puzzle below.

ACROSS

1. You can not see the cirtians from the street when I close the shutters.
2. She walked out onto the balcony and closed the shudders.
3. The flower pots sat against the windowpain on the windowsill.
4. "Don't pull the brind, I want to see the grass," said Tom.
5. The grass comes up to the padio.

DOWN

4. A lovely window pox hangs on the windowsill.
6. There was an antenna and a chimnee on the roof.
7. The rouf on the shed is black.
8. The guttar came down near the garage.
9. The garaje has a small window above the door.
10. You can see the shed from the dore.

8
1 CURTAINS
6
2
7
9
3
4
10
5

26

A House

■ ■ Use the following words to fill in the blanks in the story below. Not all of the words will be used.

doormat	**roof**	**window**	**drainpipe**	**aerial**
shutters	**door**	**walls**	**blinds**	**grass**
garage	**balcony**	**windowpanes**	**house**	**windowsills**
curtains	**shed**	**patio**		

A NEW HOUSE

Nancy and Bob live in a lovely new h o u s e. Both the r __ o __ and the __ h __ t __ e __ __ are red, and the outside __ a __ l s are white. The __ a __ c __ n __, which is directly above the __ a __ i __, is yellow. Throughout the house the __ u __ t a __ __ s are green, and the b __ i __ __ s have a floral design on them. There is a small __ __ r __ g __ next to the house which is about the same size as the neighbor's red s __ e __. The __ r __ s __ around the house is very green. The __ i __ d __ w boxes on the __ i __ d __ __ s __ l __ s make the house look very attractive. Nancy and Bob like their home very much. And if you knock on their __ o __ r, they will be very happy to show you their new house!

■ ■ ■ Now write four or five sentences about your own home or apartment.

27 The Weather / The Yard

■ ■ Use the following words to fill in the blanks in the paragraphs below. Not all of the words will be used.

sky	**leaves**	**flower pot**	**clothesline**	**snowman**
flowers	**lawn**	**branches**	**gate**	**sun**
icicle	**rain**	**bush**	**yard**	**storm**
snow	**tree**	**laundry**	**twigs**	**cloud**

It is winter. There is s n o w on the ground. The children are making a ________ in our back ________. There is an ________ hanging from the roof.

It is spring. It is dark outside. Maybe it will ________ today. That will help the ________ grow, but we will not be able to hang out the ________ on the ________ to dry.

It is summer. The ________ is shining. The ________ is blue. There is not a ________ up above. I don't think we will have a ________.

It is fall. The ________ are falling from the big ________. The wind blows many ________ and ________ to the ground. The ________ is turning brown.

28 The Hall

■ ■ Use the following words to fill in the blanks below. You will not use all of the words.

mail slot	**dial**	**lights**	**hook**	**floor**
banister	**cord**	**mat**	**rack**	**switch**
upstairs	**receiver**	**phone**	**stair**	**bolt**
telephone book	**hinge**	**rug**		

1. You use it to turn on the light. s (w) i t c h
2. You find names and numbers in it. ◯ _ _ _ _ _ _ _ _ _ _ _ _ _
3. You turn it to get a telephone number. _ _ _ ◯
4. You put it to your ear to hear a voice. _ _ ◯ _ _ _ _ _
5. You step on it to go upstairs. _ _ _ _ _
6. Letters enter the house through it. _ _ _ _ _ _ _ _
7. You hang a coat on it. _ _ _ _
8. It covers the floor. _ _ _
9. You hold on to it when you climb the stairs. _ _ _ _ _ _ _ _
10. It is the opposite of the ceiling. _ _ ◯ _ _
11. You wipe your feet on it. ◯ _ _
12. Doors hang on it. _ _ _ _ ◯

Now that you have completed the answers, put the circled letters into the puzzle to discover a new word.

PUZZLE: This word is often written on the door mat. (w) ◯ ◯ ◯ ◯ ◯ ◯

29 The Living Room

■ Circle the word that completes the sentence correctly and put it into the crossword puzzle below.

ACROSS

1. The (turntable, amplifier) makes music sound louder.
2. A (couch, drape) is to sit on.
3. A (bookcase, magazine) is to read.
4. A (shelf, drape) is to put things on.
5. The lamp is on the (end table, armchair).

DOWN

1. Put your cigarette in the (ashtray, speaker).
2. The (ceiling, cushion) is the opposite of the floor.
6. The (mantel, carpet) is over the fireplace.
7. A (wall, fire) burns in the fireplace.

1
AMPLIFIER
2
6
3
4
7
5

30 The Kitchen

■ Match the following words to make combinations that are found in the kitchen.

sugar	shaker
coffee	bowl
place	towel
napkin	pan
tea	kettle
garbage	can
pepper	pot
dish	holder
can	mat
fruit	basket
bread	box
frying	opener

■ ■ ■ Try to use each of these combinations in a sentence below.

1. **Please put the sugar bowl on the table.**
2. ______
3. ______
4. ______
5. ______
6. ______
7. ______
8. ______
9. ______
10. ______
11. ______
12. ______

30 The Kitchen

■ ■ ■ Get together with another student in the class. Pretend that you are both at the kitchen table for a meal. Write a short dialog using as many of the words below as possible. Ask your teacher how to spell new words that you want to use.

toaster	**stove**	**pan**
refrigerator	**burner**	**chair**
fruit	**counter**	**table**
coffee pot	**pot**	**dishwasher**

A KITCHEN CONVERSATION

Name: ____________________

Name: ____________________

____

____

____

____

■ ■ ■ In one paragraph describe the place setting that you see below.

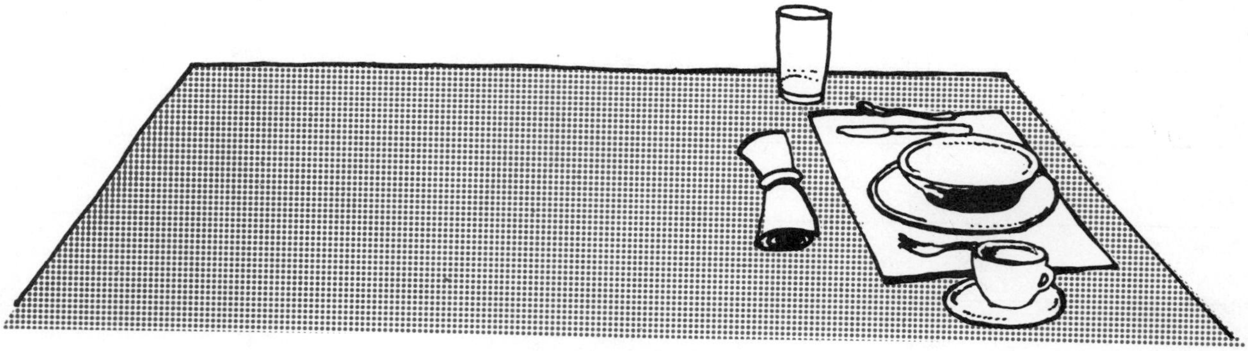

BREAKFAST

I put out the same place setting for breakfast every morning. First, I put out

____________________. Then, I

____________________. Finally,

____

Breakfast is my favorite meal!

31 Household Objects

■ It often takes two household objects to do a job. Match the following objects that go together.

scrub brush	socket
dust brush	dustpan
washing machine	scouring powder
plug	pail
iron	soap powder
mop	ironing board

■ ■ Use ten of the fifteen words below and the following clues and rhymes to find the correct household objects.

bulb	**soap**	**iron**	**hair dryer**	**pail**
plug	**mop**	**dustcloth**	**broom**	**dustpan**
vacuum cleaner	**switch**	**washing machine**	**cord**	**dust brush**

1. It sweeps the floor and rhymes with room. ____________________
2. It is long and thin and rhymes with board. ____________________
3. It turns on lights and rhymes with rich. ____________________
4. It is used after a shampoo and rhymes with fire. ____________________
5. It washes the floor and rhymes with top. ____________________
6. It holds water and rhymes with sale. ____________________
7. It goes into a socket and rhymes with rug. ____________________
8. It holds dust and dirt and rhymes with man. ____________________
9. It is sometimes a powder and rhymes with hope. ____________________
10. It makes clothes clean and rhymes with seen. ____________________

32 The Bedroom / The Baby

- Put the following words into the correct categories below. You will not use all of the words.

alarm clock	**diaper**	**night table**	**hair brush**	**sheet**
stool	**bedspread**	**doll**	**changing table**	**stuffed animal**
pillowcase	**sleeper**	**blanket**	**game**	**dressing table**
desk	**crib**	**chest of drawers**	**bib**	**bed**
rattle				

BEDCLOTHES

FURNITURE

TOYS

BABY CLOTHES

32 The Bedroom / The Baby

■ ■ Use the following words to fill in the blanks in the paragraphs below. Not all of the words will be used.

powder	**rug**	**toy**	**box**	**baby**
tissues	**crib**	**doll**	**stuffed**	**pacifier**
rattle	**bottle**	**bed**	**game**	**comb**
bib	**bedroom**	**diaper**	**desk**	**drawers**

BIG BROTHER

Jimmy shares his b e d r o o m with his baby brother Tommy. The _ _ b _ sleeps in a _ _ i _ near Jimmy's _ e _. When the baby cries, Jimmy finds a _ _ y in the toy _ o _ to quiet his brother. Sometimes he shakes a _ _ t _ _ e. Other times he tries to give Tommy his favorite soft _ _ u _ _ _ d animal, and when that doesn't work, Jimmy puts the _ _ c _ f _ _ _ in Tommy's mouth. Now and then, Jimmy has to change his brother's _ _ a _ e _ when it is wet. He likes the smell of the baby _ _ w _ _ _ that his mother tells him to put on his brother. He also helps feed the baby by putting on Tommy's _ i _ and holding up the _ _ t t _ _ for him to drink.

Jimmy has his own things in the bedroom too. He has a small chest of _ r _ _ _ _ _ where he keeps some clothing and he has a _ _ s _ where he studies. Often, while the baby plays with a _ o _ _, Jimmy plays a _ _ m _ on the _ u _. Jimmy is a big help to his parents.

33 The Bathroom

■ ■ ■ Some words look alike or almost the same. Just one letter is different. Change one letter in each underlined word to make a new word.

Change:

1. something you wear on your head (hat) to something you put on the bathroom floor:

   m a t

2. something you do with your hands (rub) to something you get into to take a bath:

   ___ ___ ___

3. something you do when you're happy (sing) to something you put water into when you wash your face:

   ___ ___ ___ ___

4. something you use to cover the floor (rug) to a cup you use for shaving:

   ___ ___ ___

5. something a teacher stands in front of (class) to something you use to drink from:

   ___ ___ ___ ___ ___

6. something you eat (soup) to something you use to wash your hands:

   ___ ___ ___ ___

7. something hard on the ground (rock) to something you hang towels on:

   ___ ___ ___ ___

8. something clocks tell us (time) to something you use to cover bathroom walls:

   ___ ___ ___ ___

9. something a thief does (rob) to something you hang shower curtains on:

   ___ ___ ___

10. something you use as a tool (hammer) to something you put dirty clothes into:

    ___ ___ ___ ___ ___ ___

33 The Bathroom

■ ■ Use the following words to fill in the blanks in the story below. Not all of the words will be used.

medicine	**plug**	**shaving**	**faucet**	**bathroom**
handle	**shower**	**bathtubs**	**water**	**mats**
glass	**head**	**razor**	**curtain**	**toilet**

A DANGEROUS PLACE

The b a t h r o o m can be a dangerous place. If there are children in the house, the _ _ d _ _ _ _ _ chest should be locked. Sharp objects such as _ _ _ o _ blades should never be out in the open. The bathroom _ _ a _ _ should be made out of plastic because it can break and cut someone. Everyone should be careful when they take showers because people often slip and fall in _ _ t h _ _ _ _ or on bath _ _ t _. Hot _ a _ e _ should not be heated too hot because people can burn themselves when they turn on the hot water _ _ u _ e _. Also children should know that it is dangerous to swing from the _ h _ w _ _ _ _ r _ a _ n rod. It is best for children never to play in the bathroom.

■ ■ Now unscramble these scrambled bathroom items that are **not** dangerous.

1. coltshawh ________________
2. nopges ________________
3. wetlo ________________
4. laces ________________
5. hottobsurh ________________

34 In the Country

Fill in the following blanks using the words at the bottom of the page. After you discover the answer, put it into the crossword puzzle below. Not all of the words will be used.

EXAMPLE: A bush is to a tree as a baseball is to a basketball.

ACROSS

1. A ________________ is to a mountain as a kitten is to a cat.

2. A stream is to a ________________ as a car is to a truck.

3. A ________________ is to a lake as a puppy is to a dog.

DOWN

4. A ________________ is to a city as a church is to a cathedral.

5. A path is to a ________________ as a watch is to a clock.

6. ________________ is to a forest as wool is to a carpet.

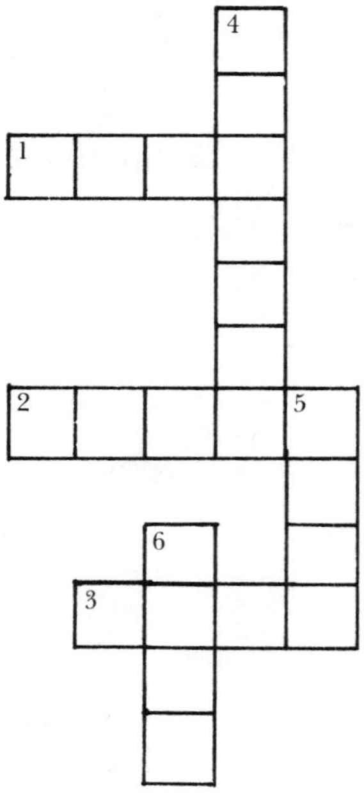
4
1
2
5
6
3

peak	**hedge**	**village**	**river**
pond	**plateau**	**wood**	**hill**
road		**field**	

34 In the Country

■ ■ Use the following words to fill in the blanks in the paragraphs below. Not all of the words will be used.

plateau	**lake**	**forests**	**fields**	**path**
mountains	**valleys**	**hills**	**hedge**	**road**
peak	**stream**	**meadow**	**village**	**pond**
waterfall	**woods**	**river**		

MOUNTAIN VIEW

Mountain View is a v i l l a g e surrounded by many high _ _ u _ _ a _ _ _, a lovely _ _ a _ o _, and a wide _ i _ e _. A nearby _ _ r _ _ _ winds through the _ _ l _ s and _ _ l _ e _ _ after it leaves a beautiful, blue _ a _ _. This lake has a _ _ _ _ r _ _ l _ running into it. There are _ o _ _ _ and _ _ r _ s _ _ among the hills, and they make the area look green. Beyond the mountains is a high _ _ a _ _ a _.

Although the village of Mountain View is very small, there is a _ _ a _ running by it. People have their farm _ i _ _ d _ behind their houses. There is a narrow _ _ t _ leading to some of these fields. Around each field is a low _ e _ _ _. Some people fish in the tiny _ _ n _ across the road from the village. Mountain View is a charming place to live.

35 Camping and at the Seaside

Which word does **not** belong to the group? Underline the one which does **not** fit. Be ready to give reasons for your answers.

1. snorkel flipper goggles <u>kite</u> **It is not used in the water.**
2. seaweed sleeping bag tent camp stove ____________
3. bucket shovel rocks beach ball ____________
4. cottage hotel sandcastle tent ____________
5. cliff wave water surf ____________
6. swimmer boardwalk sunbather ____________
7. pebbles seashells rocks backpack ____________
8. groundcloth ice cream beach towel ____________
9. motorboat beach umbrella deck chair windbreaker ____________
10. bathing trunks sunbather bathing suit ____________

A person who likes to swim is a swimmer. Discover who the following people are.

1. What is a person who likes to surf called? ____________
2. What is a person who likes to sunbathe called? ____________
3. What is a person who likes to camp called? ____________
4. What is a person who likes to boat called? ____________
5. What is a person who likes to backpack called? ____________

36 On the Farm

■ ■ Use the following words to fill in the blanks. You will not use all of the words.

rooster	**field**	**orchard**	**barnyard**	**chick**
farm house	**plow**	**wheat**	**bull**	**lamb**
hoof	**mane**	**tractor**	**saddle**	**hayloft**
pen	**duckling**	**irrigation canal**	**scarecrow**	**pond**
furrow	**barn**	**calf**	**hen**	

1. A cow lives in a (an) ____**barn**____.
2. A female chicken is a (an) ________________.
3. A combine cuts ________________.
4. A cow's baby is a (an) ________________.
5. Put the hay in the ________________.
6. A pig lives in a (an) ________________.
7. A chick's father is a (an) ________________.
8. Wheat grows in a (an) ________________.
9. The hair on a horse's neck is its ________________.
10. A (an) ________________ brings water to the fields.
11. A baby duck is a (an) ________________.
12. Ducks and chickens live in a (an) ________________.
13. A baby chicken is a (an) ________________.
14. A farmer lives in a (an) ________________.
15. A plow makes a (an) ________________.
16. You need a (an) ________________ to ride a horse.
17. A baby sheep is a (an) ________________.
18. A calf's father is a (an) ________________.
19. A fruit tree grows in a (an) ________________.
20. A horse's foot is a (an) ________________.

36 On the Farm

■ ■ Find ten misspelled words in the following paragraph. Underline them and write them correctly at the bottom of the page.

The Adams family lives on a <u>wheet</u> farm. They also have a small orcherd of peach trees. They keep animals too. They have chickins, cows, gotes, horses, and ducks. Of all the animals, Mr. Adams likes his prize bull, Harry, the best. Mrs. Adams likes Charlie the roster because each morning he wakes up everyone in the farm house. Their children, Andy and Cindy, like the horse named Sandy best of all. He takes them out on rides beyond the bond and the fense and into the feilds. Today Mr. Adams is driving the tracter and pulling the plow. He will soon plant a new crop. Andy and Cindy are riding out to bring him his lunch. As they pass the scareclow they laugh. He doesn't scare them! Life on a farm is a lot of fun.

1. wheat ________
2. ________
3. ________
4. ________
5. ________
6. ________
7. ________
8. ________
9. ________
10. ________

■ ■ ■ Write your own sentences. Choose any three of the above words and write one sentence using **all** three.

____

____

37 Power

■ Look at the picture for each sentence and then write the missing word in the crossword puzzle below.

ACROSS

1.  is a black, hard fuel.

2. A very high 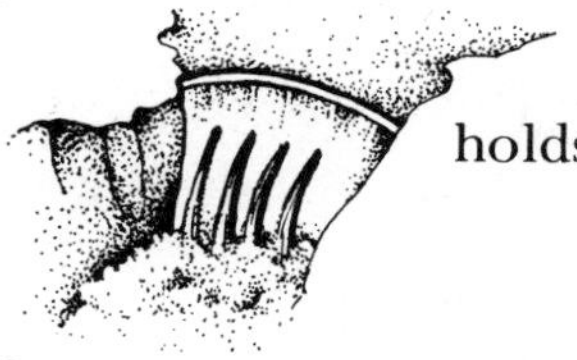 holds back water.

3. A 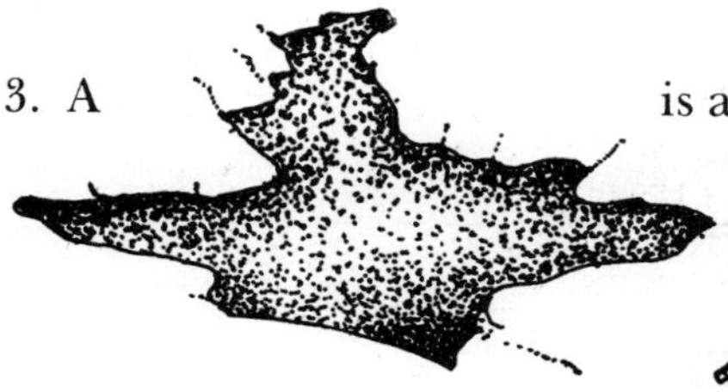 is a man-made lake.

4. The wires were held up by 

5. Oil is made more pure at a 

6. A 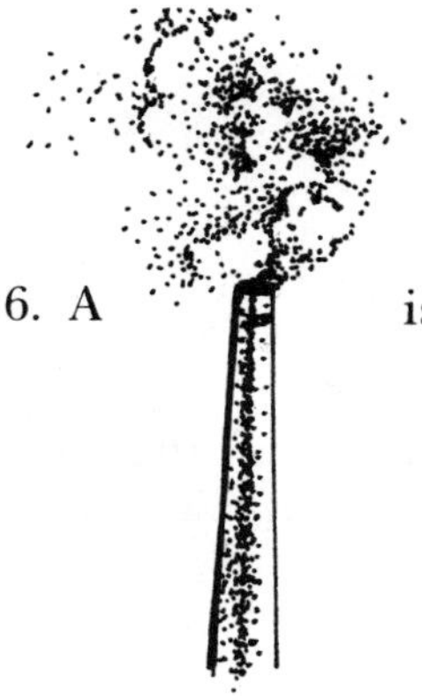 is a tall chimney.

DOWN

2. The workers built a  over the oil well.

4. A  carries oil or gas for long distances.

7. A  tank holds lots of oil.

8. Power is generated or made in a 

9. A 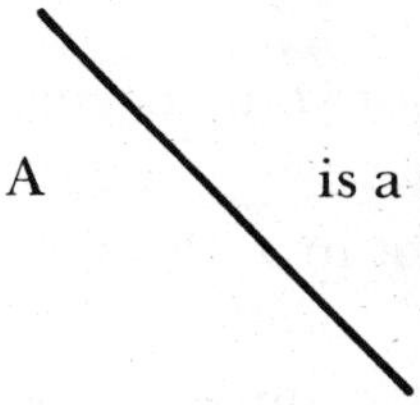 is a thick wire rope.

38 Travel by Road

■ ■ ■ Many things can go wrong with a car. Are you a good mechanic? Fill in the blanks below to find out what is wrong with your car.

1. The car behind you can't see you very well at night. You had better change the

t a i l l i g h t s.

2. The car behind you can't see that you are turning a corner. You had better fix the

_ _ (◯) _ _ _ _ _ _ _.

3. It is raining and you can't see out very well. You had better fix the

_ _ _ _ _ _ _ _ (◯) _ _ _ _ _ _ _ _ s.

4. You can't tell how fast the car is going. You had better fix the _ (◯) _ _ _ _ _ _ _ _ _ _ _.

5. You can't stop your car very quickly. You had better fix the _ _ _ _ _ s.

6. You can't put your car into reverse. You had better fix the _ _ (◯) _ _ _ _ _ _ _.

7. You can't turn the key to start your engine. You had better fix the _ _ _ _ _ _ _ _ _ _ _.

8. Your car engine gets very hot in a very short time. You had better fix the _ _ _ (◯) _ _ _ _.

9. None of your car lights will go on and your engine is dead. You had better change the

_ _ _ _ _ _ _ _ _ _.

10. You can't drive very smoothly. The car jerks. You had better change the

_ _ _ (◯) _ _ _ _ _ _ s.

11. The car coming toward you can't see you very well at night. You had better change the

_ _ _ _ _ _ _ _ _ _ _ _ _ s.

12. The radio in your car doesn't work well. You had better fix the _ _ _ _ _ _ _ _ _ _.

Now, put the circled letters into the puzzle to find a new word.

PUZZLE: What is another word for fix? (◯)(◯)(◯)(◯)(◯)(◯)

38 Travel by Road

■ ■ Find eight misspelled words in the following paragraph. Underline them and write them correctly at the bottom of the page.

Mr. Andrews had an accident with his new station wagen. His accelerater did not work correctly and he hit the sports coupe in front of him. Luckily he had his safety belt on, but the lady in front of him did not. She hit the steering wheel and her passenger hit the dashbord and windsheild. They were not too badly hurt. The cars were not as lucky as the people. The trunk and bumber of the coupe were completely smashed. The exaust system will have to be replaced. On the station wagon, the grill, headlights, and enjine were ruined. If anything like this ever happens again, Mr. Andrews says he will use his emergency blake. Until his car is repaired, he will have to use his wife's sedan.

1. wagon ______
2. ______
3. ______
4. ______
5. ______
6. ______
7. ______
8. ______

■ ■ ■ Have you ever been in an accident? Write a few sentences about your experience. Perhaps you could describe an accident that you have seen.

______

______

______

______

39 Travel by Road

Look at the pictures and put these words in the right order to make a correct sentence.

1. 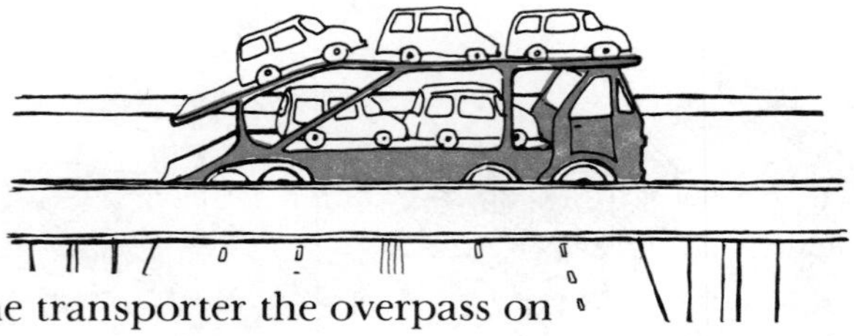

is the transporter the overpass on

The transporter is on the overpass.

2. 

the sports front the in is of ambulance car

3. 

one station there car the at is gas

4. 

truck the behind transporter trailer the is

5. 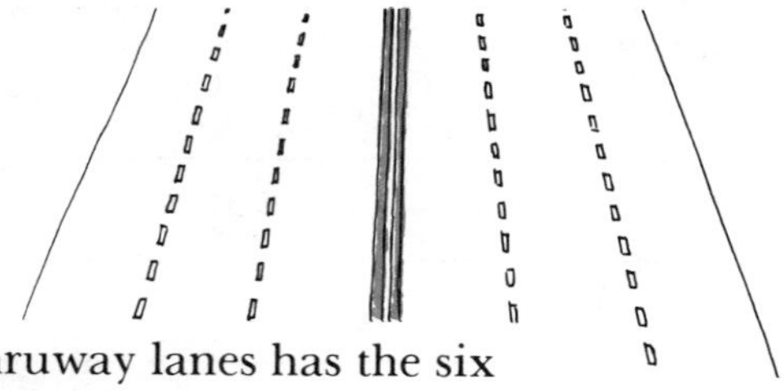

thruway lanes has the six

6. 

lane in is motorcycle the the left

7. 

passing bus the car the is sports

8. 

pump the in attendant of gas front the is

9. 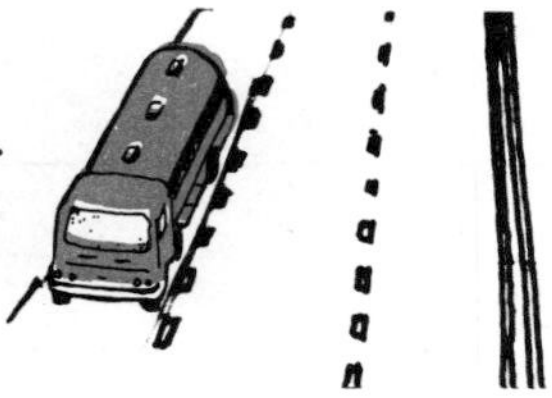

is truck the in lane oil the inside

10. 

van behind the is car the

40 Travel by Road

■ Make seven new words by matching the following words. Draw a line between the words which go together.

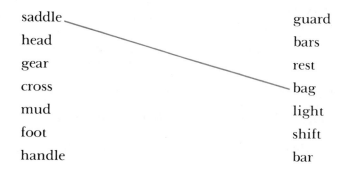

saddle	guard
head	bars
gear	rest
cross	bag
mud	light
foot	shift
handle	bar

■ ■ Which word does **not** belong to the group? Underline the one which does **not** fit. Be ready to give reasons for your answers.

1. crash helmet <u>cable</u> goggles You don't wear a cable.

2. rear light reflector spokes headlight ______

3. seat passenger taxi driver ______

4. valve spokes accelerator ______

5. motor scooter bicycle taxi ______

6. pump meter fare ______

41 Travel by Train

■ ■ Using ten of the fifteen words below, fill in the blank spaces. The following clues and rhymes will help you.

gate	**ticket**	**seat**	**conductor**	**coach**
engineer	**ties**	**platform**	**luggage rack**	**siding**
buffer	**flag**	**track**	**switch**	**engine**

1. He drives a train and rhymes with ear. ______________________
2. You put suitcases on it and it rhymes with back. ______________________
3. It pulls the train and it rhymes with pin. ______________________
4. He collects the tickets and rhymes with her. ______________________
5. You go through this to catch the train and it rhymes with late. ______________
6. The train rides on this and it rhymes with sack. ______________________
7. It changes the train to another track and it rhymes with which. ______________
8. You stand on this to catch the train and it rhymes with warm. ______________
9. The brakeman waves this and it rhymes with bag. ______________________
10. These are under the tracks and they rhyme with buys. ______________________

ON THE TRAIN

■ ■ ■ Get together with another student in the class. Pretend that one of you is the train conductor and the other a passenger. Write a short dialog using as many of the words below as possible. Ask your teacher to help you spell new words that you want to use.

ticket	**seat**	**compartment**	**whistle**
train	**schedule**	**luggage rack**	**station**

Conductor: ____

Passenger: ____

Conductor: ____

Passenger: ____

42

Travel by Water

■ ■ Use the following words to fill in the blanks below. Then put the words into the crossword puzzle. You will not use all of the words.

horizon	**wharf**	**hold**	**buoy**	**windlass**
pier	**cargo**	**gangway**	**bollard**	**forklift**
crane	**anchor**	**dock**	**cable**	

ACROSS

1. A c a b l e is a very strong rope.
2. A _________ has four wheels and picks up heavy loads.
3. Tie the ship to the _________ on the wharf.
4. The products that a ship carries is called its ______.
5. A ______ is small and floats in the water.

DOWN

6. The _________ is where the sky and water meet.
7. The _______ is where the ship loads and unloads.
8. A person can walk a long way out into the water on a _____.
9. Drop the ship's _______ when you want to stop.
10. Put the cargo below in the ship's _____.

7
8
6
1 CABLE
2
3
9
10
4
5

43 Travel by Water

■ ■ ■ Some words look alike or almost the same. Just one letter is different. Change one letter in each underlined word to make a new word.

Change:

1. something that a car pulls (trailer) to a kind of fishing boat. (t) r a w l e r

2. a small amount of water (puddle) to something you use to steer a canoe.

   _ _ _ _ _ (_)

3. a farm animal (duck) to a place for walking on a ship. _ (_) _

4. a motor vehicle (car) to something you use to steer a rowboat. _ (_) _

5. a word that means quick (fast) to a pole that holds up the sails on a boat.

   _ _ (_)

6. another word for big (large) to a small cargo boat. _ (_) _ _ _

7. the past tense of say (said) to something that the wind uses to move a boat.

   _ (_) _

8. a kind of fruit (berry) to a small passenger boat. _ _ _ _ _

9. a farm animal (cow) to the front of a boat. _ _ _

10. the back of your foot (heel) to a part of the bottom of a boat. _ _ _ _

Now that you have completed all the answers, put the circled letters into the following puzzle to discover a new word.

PUZZLE: Who is the person who runs a ship? (t) h (_) (_)(_) p (_)(_)(_) n

44 Travel by Air

Use the following words to fill in the blanks in the paragraph below. Not all of the words will be used.

airport	**hangar**	**tail**
control	**propeller**	**steward**
airplane	**passenger**	**fuselage**
luggage	**customs**	**runway**
stewardess	**rotor**	**passport**
officer	**pilot**	**engine**

AN AIRPORT

An — — — — — — — is a busy place. Many people work there. For example, if you are coming from a foreign country, you will have to go through — — — — — — — and show your — — — — — — — — to a customs — — — — — — — —. Also many people work in the — — — — — — — tower to help guide — — — — — — — — s down the — — — — — —. Many people also work in the — — — — — — where they repair planes and make sure that the jet — — — — — — s are working well. Of course, there are workers inside of the planes too. Men, called — — — — — — — s, and women, called — — — — — — — — — — e s, help the — — — — — — — — s to be comfortable. They also help them with any extra — — — — — — — that they have. However, the most important person working on the plane is the — — — — —. All of the workers at an airport help to make flying a safe and easy way to travel.

45 National Defense

■ Put the following words into the correct categories below. Two of the words will **not** fit into any category.

bomber	**cockpit**	**submarine**	**revolver**	**aircraft carrier**
jeep	**warship**	**rifle**	**soldier**	**navigator**
parachute	**tank**	**fighter plane**	**bayonet**	**pistol**
grenade	**pilot**	**machine gun**		

PEOPLE	**WEAPONS**	**VEHICLES**
________	________	________
________	________	________
________	________	________
	________	________
	________	________
	________	________
		________

Which are the two words that you did not use? ________

____

■ ■ ■ Take any three words that you have used on this page and use them in a sentence below.

____

____

____

46–48

Recreation: Sport

■ ■ Look at the scrambled words and the following clues and guess the correct sport.

1. You play this game on a table. gnip-nogp ____________________
2. You must be very strong in this sport. tlerwings ____________________
3. You use poles to travel down a mountain in this sport. nikgis ____________________
4. You need a rod, hook and line to enjoy this sport. nisfhig ____________________
5. You wear a helmet in this sport. oblaflot ____________________
6. Jockeys wear jodhpurs and caps when they enjoy this sport. nicgar ____________________
7. You wear a white suit when you enjoy this sport. oduj ____________________
8. You use a stick in this sport. yoheck ____________________
9. You hit the ball with a large racket in this game. nisent ____________________
10. You hit the ball with a bat in this sport. eblasbla ____________________
11. Another name for ping-pong is balte-ntines. ____________________
12. You put the ball through a net in this sport. staklableb ____________________
13. You wear special shoes with blades on the bottom for this sport.

    cie-taksing ____________________
14. You wear gloves in this sport. gonixb ____________________

46-48

Recreation: Sport

■ Match the words from the same sport.

1. hook	j	**a. table**
2. service line	______	**b. bridle**
3. boxer	______	**c. pole**
4. goalpost	______	**d. backboard**
5. reins	______	**e. pitcher**
6. ping-pong	______	**f. field hockey**
7. home plate	______	**g. glove**
8. ski	______	**h. football**
9. basket	______	**i. tennis ball**
10. stick	______	**j. line**

■ ■ ■ Who is your favorite sports star? Write a short paragraph about him or her. Give the answers to these questions in the paragraph.

1. What sport does he or she play?
2. What country is he or she from?
3. What makes this person so popular?

A STAR ATHLETE

46-48

Recreation: Sport

Which word does **not** belong to the group? Underline the one which does **not** fit. Be ready to give reasons for your answers.

1. tennis baseball horse racing ______ **A ball is not used.** ______
2. judo boxing baseball wrestling ______
3. tobogganist fisherman skier ______
4. bridle net bit stirrup ______
5. field hockey baseball basketball ice-skating ______
6. scoreboard stick racket bat ______
7. first baseman center fielder bat shortstop ______
8. fishing racing skiing basketball ______
9. boxing glove helmet mitt ______
10. tennis judo ping-pong ______
11. fullback right tackle boxer center ______
12. pitcher jockey catcher left fielder ______
13. boxing basketball tennis ping-pong ______
14. basketball football baseball ______
15. saddle court ring field ______

49 Recreation: Music

■ ■ Look at the following words and do the puzzles below. There is a small word within each larger vocabulary word. Not all of the words will be used.

conductor	**clarinet**	**rostrum**	**trumpet**	**pedal**
baton	**trombone**	**horn**	**cello**	**cymbals**
slide	**piano**	**strings**	**drum**	**mouthpiece**
stool				

1. You see the word tool, but it doesn't help you work. You sit on it. What is it? stool

2. You see the word ring, but it isn't jewelry. It's a part of a violin. What is it? ____________

3. You see the word bone, but it isn't a part of the body. It's a musical instrument that is blown. What is it? ____________

4. You see the word rum, but it isn't a drink. It's a musical instrument that is hit. What is it? ____________

5. You see the word ton, but it isn't heavy. A conductor uses it. What is it? ____________

6. You see the word pet, but it isn't an animal. It's a musical instrument that is blown. What is it? ____________

7. You see the word lid, but it doesn't cover anything. It's a part of a trombone. What is it? ____________

8. You see the word net, but it doesn't catch anything. It's a musical instrument that is blown. What is it? ____________

9. You see the word no, but it isn't the opposite of yes. It's a very large musical instrument. What is it? ____________

10. You see the word pie, but it isn't something to eat. It's a part of a musical instrument. What is it? ____________

49 Recreation: Music

■ Put the following words into the correct categories below. Some of the words will **not** fit into any category.

viola	**player**	**violin**	**double bass**	**trumpet**
microphone	**speaker**	**trombone**	**singer**	**drum**
horn	**saxophone**	**musician**	**conductor**	**cello**
guitar	**cymbals**	**music**		

STRINGED INSTRUMENTS

PERCUSSION INSTRUMENTS

WIND INSTRUMENTS

PEOPLE

■ ■ ■ Which are the words that you did not use? Use at least two of them in a sentence below.

50 Recreation: Leisure

Often you can tell a lot about a person if you know how they spend their leisure time. Answer the following questions in complete sentences. Be ready to share your answers with the class.

1. Who is your favorite actor? ______________________________

2. Who is your favorite actress? ______________________________

3. What is the best movie you have ever seen? ______________________________

____

4. Have you ever seen a stage play? If so, what was the play, and where did you see it?

____

____

5. Have you ever gone to a concert? If so, which one? ______________________________

____

6. What was the title of the last book that you have read? ______________________________

____

7. Where is the closest library to your house? ______________________________

____

8. What kind of books do you like? ______________________________

____

9. How often do you watch TV? ______________________________

____

10. What kind of TV shows do you like? ______________________________

____

11. Have you ever seen TV programs from other countries? Which ones? ______________

____

12. Does TV in your home country have commercials? ______________________________

____

50 Recreation: Leisure

■ ■ Use the following words to fill in the blanks in the paragraph below. Not all of the words will be used.

gallery	**usherette**	**actor**	**seats**	**stage**
screen	**curtain**	**movies**	**actress**	**movie theater**
wings	**aisle**	**projector**	**balcony**	**spotlight**
orchestra				

AT THE MOVIES

Mike and Patty go to the m o v i e s often. They like to sit in the _ _ l _ _ n _ where they are not so close to the _ c _ _ _ _. They usually choose _ _ a _ _ next to the _ _ s _ _ so that they can get out of the _ o _ _ _ _ h _ _ _ _ _ quickly after the show is over. Last night they went to see a movie with their favorite _ c _ _ _ _ _ and _ _ _ o _ in it. The _ _ _ _ a _ _ went up and the movie began. After about ten minutes, the movie stopped. Everyone in the audience wondered what had happened. In a while, one of the _ _ h _ _ _ _ _ _ s came out from the _ _ n _ _ of the _ _ a _ _. There was a _ _ o _ _ i _ _ _ on her. She said that the _ _ _ _ e _ _ _ _ had broken, but everyone would get tickets for the next night. Mike and Patty can't go to the movies tonight. They're angry!

51 Recreation: Bar/Restaurant

■ Put the following words into the correct categories below.

jigger	soft drink	wine	cocktail waitress	customer
can	ashtray	corkscrew	bottle	wine glass
waiter	bartender	draft beer	bottle opener	hard liquor
pepper shaker	mug	lighter	saltshaker	
straw	pepper mill			

PEOPLE

____

____

____

____

TOOLS

____

____

____

____

LIQUIDS

____

____

____

____

CONTAINERS

____

____

____

____

____

____

____

____

____

■ ■ ■ Get together with another student in the class and write a short dialog between a customer and a waiter or waitress in a restaurant.

Customer: _______________________

Waiter/Waitress: _______________________

Customer: _______________________

Waiter/Waitress: _______________________

51 Recreation: Bar/Restaurant

■ ■ ■ Fill in the following blanks. Then find the words in the puzzle below. Some words go across and others go down.

ACROSS

1. Sit at the bar on a s t o o l.
2. Use a _ _ _ _ _ _ _ _ _ to get out the cork from a bottle of wine.
3. Pay the _ _ _ _ _ before you leave the restaurant.
4. Pass the _ _ _ _ _ _ _ _ _ _ _. The food is not salty enough.
5. Drink a soft drink through a _ _ _ _ _.

DOWN

1. Whiskey is a kind of _ _ _ _ _ _.
2. You get draft beer from a _ _ _.
3. Put the _ _ _ in the ashtray.
4. All of the food is listed on the _ _ _ _.
5. The _ _ _ _ _ _ _ _ waitress serves drinks from the bar.

```
C N U R T X O B T E K S A B L E C A B N A C H S A R T
E A W C N O Y R A C E S A C T I O G N I P O H S E T A
A S A L T S H A K E R G A L B N C R A G C I T S A L P
I U S L A P A R W S O M R I E H K U C R E P A P N A C
S N H N E T L L A B T E K Q C A T C H E C K I O F M U
M F T F E L R E T T A B R U I P A R E H S I F T R U O
E L D A S P U R I N A M E O S A I N O C E S R E D T L
N L G N I X O B E T S S T R A W L F E R S R U P H A D
U E L T S E R W E L D I R B S N E D R A O B K C A P B
L O G S T O O L N A G O B O T K A R E T R A U Q O D U
M C O L R A D S S A L D N I W K A S C O R K S C R E W
```

52

Recreation: Hobbies

■ Read the following sentences. Underline the word that is misspelled in each sentence. Correct the spelling and write the correctly spelled word in the crossword puzzle below.

ACROSS

1. Many books have dust jackets over their covers and spins.
2. She has a roll of film, a camera and a rens in her camera bag.
3. Both checkers and chest are played on a board.
4. Ask the photografer to give me a negative of that photo.
5. I can see that you have mostly diomonds and spades in your hand and almost no hearts and clubs.

DOWN

4. The bawn, rook, knight, bishop, queen and king are parts of a chess set.
5. In every dack of cards there is only one ace of spades and one jack of clubs.
6. On the first page there were several illestrations to help in understanding the text.
7. Photography is a wonderful hoby if you have an interest in cameras and film.
8. Put the projecter on the stand and get out the screen so that we can show slides.

8
1 S P 6 I N E S
2
3
4
7
5

53 Sewing and Knitting

■ Match the sewing and knitting words that go together.

1. button ____c____
2. hook ________
3. knitting needle ________
4. needle ________
5. cloth ________

a. **wool**
b. **thread**
c. **buttonhole**
d. **scissors**
e. **eye**

■ ■ Which word does **not** belong to the group? Underline the one which does **not** fit. Be ready to give reasons for your answers.

1. button   ruffle   hook and eye   snap   **It doesn't hold clothing together.**
2. knitting needle   safety pin   needle   straight pin   ________
3. lace   ribbon   thimble   ruffle   ________
4. seam   hem   pleat   sewing machine   ________
5. material   needle   pin   scissors   ________

■ ■ You have a job to do. What would you need to do the job? You may use an answer more than once.

1. Knit a sweater. ________

2. Sew on a button. ________

3. Put in a zipper. ________

4. Shorten a dress. ________

54 Occupations / Professions

■ ■ Use the following clues to unscramble the scrambled words.

1.	wolnc	This person makes you happy when you are sad.	clown
2.	trapnerec	This person makes things out of wood.	
3.	nemcicha	This person repairs your automobile.	
4.	tispyt	This person works in an office.	
5.	thucreb	This person cuts meat.	
6.	recnunoan	This person works for a radio station.	
7.	satserwi	This person serves food.	
8.	sittra	This person loves different colors.	
9.	reptor	This person carries your bags.	
10.	ramshegnolno	This person works near boats.	
11.	nirem	This person works below ground.	
12.	ksermrdaes	This person works with cloth.	

55 Occupations / Professions

■ Circle the word that completes the sentence correctly and put it into the crossword puzzle below.

ACROSS

1. A/an (salesman, optician) tests your eyes.
2. (Gardeners, policemen) plant seeds.
3. A (sailor, barber) lives on a ship.
4. A (doctor, barber) cuts hair.
5. (Florists, soldiers) carry guns.

DOWN

6. A/an (electrician, photographer) takes pictures.
7. A (teacher, salesman) sells things.
8. A (baker, nurse) gives pills.
9. (Teachers, florists) write on blackboards.
10. A (doctor, sailor) makes you well.

OPTICIAN

54 | 55

Occupations / Professions

■ ■ Which word does **not** belong to the group? Underline the one that does **not** fit. Be ready to give reasons for your answers.

1. waitress carpenter baker butcher He has nothing to do with food.
2. miner nurse doctor optician ____________________
3. sailor policeman soldier typist ____________________
4. electrician teacher carpenter ____________________
5. gardener bank teller florist ____________________
6. artist photographer redcap ____________________
7. dressmaker mechanic truck driver ____________________
8. hairdresser barber policeman ____________________
9. fruit seller clown salesman ____________________
10. bank teller typist longshoreman ____________________

■ ■ ■ What is *your* profession or occupation? In a few sentences describe what you do and why you enjoy your job. If you are a student, what do you hope to become and why?

____

____

____

____

____

What is your father's profession or occupation? ____________________

Mother's? ______________ Brother's? ______________ Sister's? ______________

Husband's/Wife's? ____________________

54 55 Occupations / Professions

■ ■ Decide who you would call if you had the following needs. Some questions may have more than one answer.

Who would you call:

1. if you needed bread? a baker ______
2. if you were sick? ______
3. if you needed a new skirt? ______
4. if you wanted your picture taken? ______
5. if you needed some bananas? ______
6. if you wanted service in a restaurant? ______
7. if your house were robbed? ______
8. if you wanted to know the news? ______
9. if you wanted to take a class? ______
10. if your car wouldn't run? ______
11. if the lights in your house went out? ______
12. if you wanted to build a new house? ______
13. if you needed new glasses? ______
14. if you wanted a shampoo and set? ______
15. if you wanted flowers for your wife? ______
16. if you wanted a ship unloaded? ______
17. if you needed a new stove? ______
18. if your secretary quit? ______
19. if you wanted some steaks for a party? ______
20. if you wanted a painting of your daughter? ______

56 Animals

■ ■ Look at the following words and do the puzzles below. There is a small word within each larger vocabulary word. Not all of the words will be used.

rabbit	**squirrel**	**snout**	**whisker**	**kitten**
puppy	**camel**	**hump**	**donkey**	**hedgehog**
antler	**mouse**			

1. You see the word key, but it won't open a door. It looks like a horse. What is it?

   ____donkey____

2. You see the word ten, but it isn't a number. It's a popular pet. What is it?

   ____

3. You see the word out, but it isn't the opposite of in. It's a pig's nose. What is it?

   ____

4. You see the word his, but it isn't the opposite of her. It's near a rabbit's mouth. What is it? ________________

5. You see the word came, but it isn't the past tense of come. It doesn't need water very often. What is it? ________________

6. You see the word ant, but it isn't an insect. It's on a reindeer's head. What is it?

   ____

7. You see the word bit, but it isn't the past tense of bite. It has long ears. What is it?

   ____

8. You see the word hum, but it has nothing to do with music. It's on a camel's back. What is it? ________________

9. You see the word up, but it isn't the opposite of down. It's a young dog. What is it? ________________

10. You see the word edge, but it isn't at the end of anything. It's a spiny animal. What is it? ________________

56 | 57

Animals

■ ■ Fill in the following blanks using the words at the bottom of the page. Not all of the words will be used.

1. A kitten is to a cat as a ____puppy____ is to a dog.
2. A puppy is to a dog as a ____________ is to a horse.
3. A paw is to a dog as a ____________ is to a seal.
4. A horn is to a buffalo as an antler is to a ____________.
5. Stripes are to a tiger as spots are to a ____________.
6. A ____________ is to a pig as a trunk is to an elephant.
7. A fluke is to a ____________ as a tail is to a rat.
8. A top fin is to a dolphin as a ____________ is to a camel.
9. A horn is to a rhinoceros as tusks are to an ____________.
10. Wings are to a bat as flippers are to a ____________.

leopard	**hedgehog**	**hump**	**zebra**	**reindeer**
elephant	**puppy**	**seal**	**donkey**	**snout**
flipper	**wolf**	**foal**	**whale**	

■ ■ ■ Do you have a pet? If so, use the lines below to write about it. If you don't, tell about the pet of a friend or relative.

____

____

____

____

____

58 Animals

Use the following words to fill in the blanks below. You will not use all of the words.

fin	**salmon**	**centipede**	**frog**	**slug**
crab	**swordfish**	**gills**	**shark**	**spider**
sunfish	**lobster**	**eel**	**tail**	**scales**
snail	**jellyfish**	**worm**	**octopus**	**scorpion**

1. It has eight arms. o c t o (p) u s
2. It can spin a web. _ _ _ _ _ _
3. It has many, many legs. _ _ _ _ _ _ _ _ _
4. It's a fish, but looks like a snake. _ (_) _
5. It has four legs and lives in water. _ _ _ _
6. It's large and dangerous to swimmers. _ _ _ _ _
7. It carries its house with it. _ _ _ _ _
8. Be careful! It has pincers! _ _ (_) _
9. It's a fish with a very sharp snout. _ _ _ _ _ _ _ _ _
10. You find these on the skin of a fish. _ _ _ _ _ _
11. Fish breathe through these. _ _ _ _ _
12. Be careful! Its tail is dangerous! _ _ _ (_) _ _ _ _
13. It's not a fish and it looks like a small snake. _ _ _ _
14. Fisherman love to catch it. It's good to eat. _ _ _ _ _ _
15. Many people think its tail is delicious. (_) _ _ _ _ _ _

Now that you have completed the answers, put the circled letters into the puzzle to discover a new word.

PUZZLE: If you are lucky you will find one in an oyster.

(p) (_) (_) (_) (_)

59 Animals

Read the following paragraph carefully. Then, answer the questions below in complete sentences.

THE INSECT COLLECTOR

Mark is a biologist who collects insects. He has a beautiful collection of butterflies and moths. It is strange that often the most beautiful butterflies and moths come from cocoons made by very ugly caterpillars. Last summer Mark added some unusual beetles, dragonflies, and grasshoppers to his collection. This year he wants to find a large mantis. It seems that some insects do not like to be collected. Last week two wasps and a bee stung him! Mosquitos and flies don't like Mark either. It can be dangerous to collect insects!

1. What kind of work does Mark do? ______________________

____

2. What kind of collection does Mark have? ______________________

____

3. What do ugly caterpillars often become? ______________________

____

4. What kind of insect is Mark looking for this year? ______________________

____

5. What happened to Mark last week? ______________________

____

60 Animals

The following statements are **not** correct. Correct them by drawing a line through the name of the bird and writing the correct bird's name on the line. There may be more than one correct answer and you may use some birds more than once.

THE WRONG BIRD

1. The ~~flamingo~~ lives in a very cold place. ____penguin____
2. The parakeet is good to eat. ________________
3. A swan can talk. ________________
4. The crow has a long neck. ________________
5. The hummingbird is the largest living bird. ________________
6. The sparrow has a beautiful tail. ________________
7. The eagle takes nectar from flowers. ________________
8. The blackbird is pink. ________________
9. The penguin is small but has long wings. ________________
10. The vulture is small and yellow and sings well. ________________
11. The dove has a crest on its head. ________________
12. The flamingo is all black. ________________
13. The heron can run very fast, but can't fly. ________________
14. The canary eats small animals. ________________
15. The swallow eats dead animals. ________________

Choose a bird that you are familiar with in your home country. Use the lines below to write about that bird.

____

____

____

____

61 Plants

■ ■ The key at the bottom of this page will help you fill in the blanks in the following recipe.

FANTASTIC FRUIT SALAD

Ingredients:

1 cup fresh __________ slices
16-5-1-3-8

1 cup seedless green ______________
7-18-1-16-5-19

1 cup fresh _________ slices
16-5-1-18

1 cup fresh ______________________________
19-20-18-1-23-2-5-18-18-9-5-19

1 cup ____________ slices
2-1-14-1-14-1

1 cup fresh ______________________ chunks
16-9-14-5-1-16-16-12-5

1 cup ______________ sections
15-18-1-14-7-5

12 lettuce leaves

½ cup chopped ___________________
23-1-12-14-21-20-19

Recipe:

Peel and slice the _______________ and _______________. Cut the ______________ and
16-5-1-3-8-5-19 · 2-1-14-1-14-1-19 · 7-18-1-16-5-19

______________________________ into halves. Prepare the ______________________ chunks and slice the
19-20-18-1-23-2-5-18-18-9-5-19 · 16-9-14-5-1-16-16-12-5

____________. Next, peel an ______________ and section it. Tear six lettuce leaves into small pieces. Mix
16-5-1-18-19 · 15-18-1-14-7-5

all of the above in a large salad bowl. Spoon some of this fruit onto the last six lettuce leaves—each on

a separate plate. Put the ___________________ on top.
23-1-12-14-21-20-19

Serve with a mixture of ¾ cup honey and two tablespoons of ______________ juice and two
12-5-13-15-14

tablespoons of ______________ juice.
15-18-1-14-7-5

Key:

A	B	C	D	E	F	G	H	I	J	K	L	M	N	O	P
1	2	3	4	5	6	7	8	9	10	11	12	13	14	15	16

Q	R	S	T	U	V	W	X	Y	Z
17	18	19	20	21	22	23	24	25	26

61 Plants

Using twelve of the fifteen words below, fill in the blank spaces. The following clues and rhymes will help you.

core	**grapefruit**	**date**	**vine**	**plum**
stone	**mango**	**cherry**	**fig**	**rind**
papaya	**peanut**	**stalk**	**pear**	**cactus**

1. It's a purple fruit and rhymes with come. ________________

2. It's small, served at parties and rhymes with cut. ________________

3. It's in the center of some fruit and rhymes with bone. ________________

4. It has many little seeds and rhymes with big. ________________

5. It's round and red and rhymes with very. ________________

6. It's the center of an apple and rhymes with four. ________________

7. Grapes grow on it and it rhymes with nine. ________________

8. It's big, round, and yellow and rhymes with boot. ________________

9. It's on the outside of an orange and rhymes with kind. ________________

10. It grows on a palm tree and rhymes with gate. ________________

11. It's soft and sweet and rhymes with a dance called the tango. ________________

12. Be careful when you touch it, because it's sharp. It rhymes with practice.

____

61–63

Plants

■ Match the name of each plant on the left with the part that belongs to it.

1. walnut	l	a. **pit**
2. pea	________	b. **petal**
3. banana	________	c. **rind**
4. peach	________	d. **stalk**
5. cherry	________	e. **ear**
6. oak	________	f. **frond**
7. orange	________	g. **pod**
8. fern	________	h. **vine**
9. pine	________	i. **needle**
10. grape	________	j. **core**
11. apple	________	k. **acorn**
12. rose	________	l. **nutmeat**
13. bean	________	m. **peel**
14. corn	________	n. **stone**

■ ■ ■ Answer these questions.

1. What is your favorite green vegetable? ________________

2. What is your favorite fruit? ________________

3. What is your favorite non-green vegetable? ________________

4. What are some vegetables that you have *never* eaten? ________________

____

5. What are some fruits that you have *never* eaten? ________________

____

62 63

Plants

■ Decide if these sentences are true or false.

	TRUE	FALSE
1. An orchid is a vegetable.		X
2. A twig is part of a branch.		
3. An onion can make you laugh.		
4. An oak is a flower.		
5. A log is a section of tree trunk.		
6. Tree roots are found above the ground.		
7. A bean is found on a stalk.		
8. Tea leaves are for making a drink.		
9. Peas are found in a petal.		
10. Cocoa beans are for making coffee.		
11. A rose is sweet to smell.		
12. There is a large pit in a potato.		
13. A tomato is round and red.		
14. There are many seeds in a sunflower.		
15. There are needles on a palm tree.		

■ Correct any five of the false sentences above by adding the word **not**. Write the new sentences below.

Example: An orchid is **not** a vegetable.

1. ______________________________
2. ______________________________
3. ______________________________
4. ______________________________
5. ______________________________

64 Verbs

■ Look at the pictures below and answer each question by using the correct verb.

1. Is the boy laughing?

No, he isn't. He's crying.

2. Are the boys driving?

3. Is the girl swimming?

4. Is the man digging?

5. Is the boy flying?

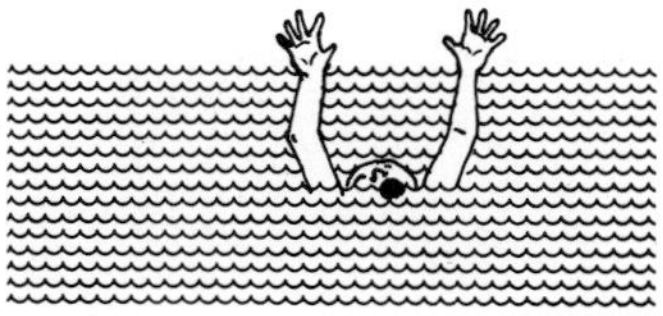

6. Is the man crawling?

7. Is the girl falling?

8. Is the girl cutting?

9. Is the child kneeling?

10. Is the child kicking a ball?

65 Verbs

■ Put these words in the right order to make a correct sentence.

1. is coffee the she stirring

She is stirring the coffee.

7. is his he washing clothes

2. cart girl is the the pulling

8. child is book the reading the

3. man the is gun shooting the

9. the is door man the pushing

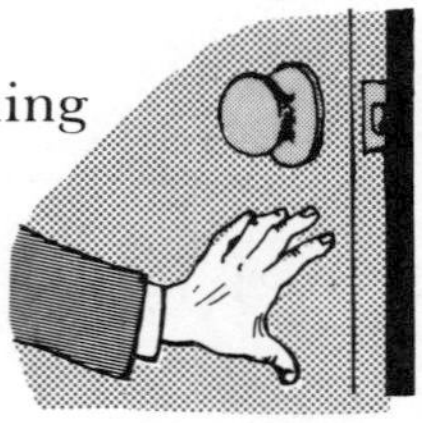

4. tying the lady is package the

10. the are boat they sailing

5. man is the door the shutting

11. woman is the paper tearing the

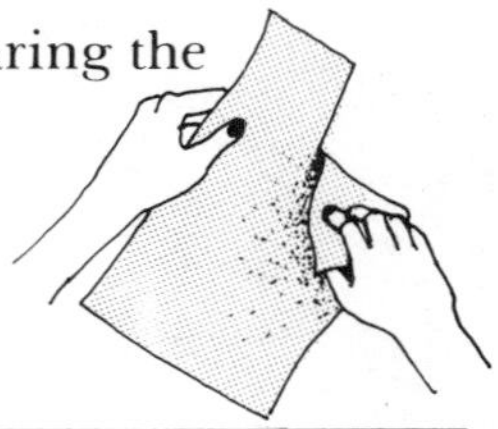

6. material sewing is she the

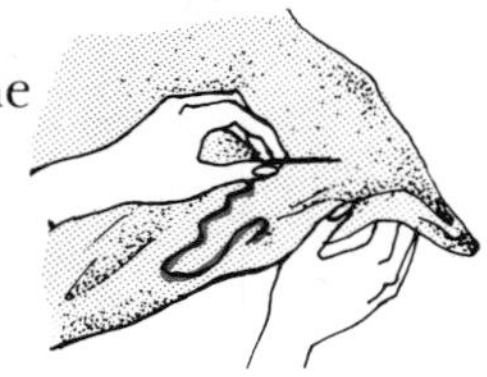

12. sweeping girl the the is floor

65 Verbs

■ Look at the following paragraph. Use the pictures to help you fill in the missing verbs.

THE BROTHERS

Jack and Fred are brothers. Jack likes to  paint

pictures and  ____________ in the park. On the other hand,

Fred likes to  ____________ horses and 

____________ races. Jack is quiet. Often he will 

____________ and  ____________ to music while his

brother Fred goes out to 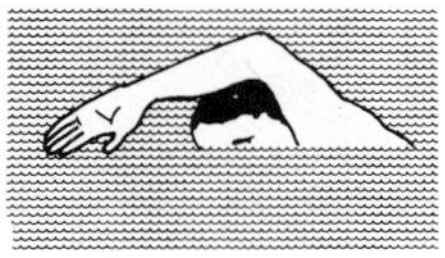 ____________ at the beach. But,

there is one thing that both boys like to do. Jack and Fred like to 

____________ together. For brothers, they are very different.

■ ■ Complete the short paragraph below. Now tell about things that **you** like to do.

I like to ____________________ and ____________________.

I also like to ____.

I am a ____________________ person.
(quiet/active)

66 Verbs

■ ■ Look at the pictures and use the following words to make sentences of your own.

the flower	**a letter**	**the wood**	**the drum**	**the truck**
her hand	**his shirt**	**his watch**	**the wheel**	**the package**
her hair	**the paper**	**his wife**	**his hands**	**the ball**

1.  She is waving her hand.

2.  ______________________

3.  ______________________

4.  ______________________

5.  ______________________

6.  ______________________

7.  ______________________

8.  ______________________

9.  ______________________

10.  ______________________

11.  ______________________

12.  ______________________

13.  ______________________

14.  ______________________

15.  ______________________

66 Verbs

Look at the pictures below and then find the verbs in the following puzzle. Some words go down, some across, and some diagonal.

1.

2.

3.

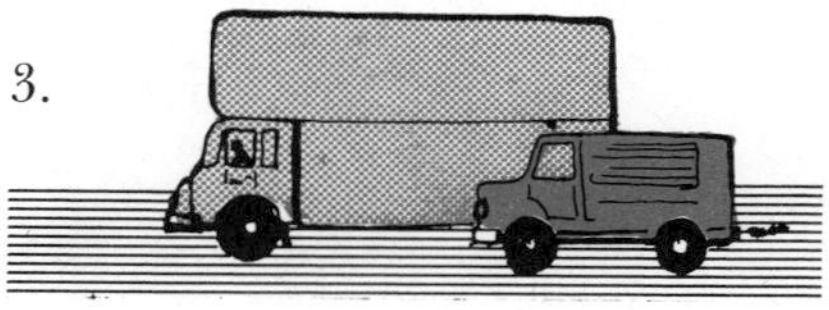

4.

5.

6.

7.

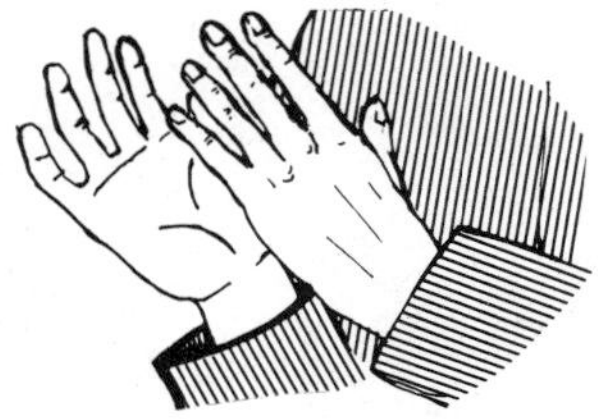

8.

9.

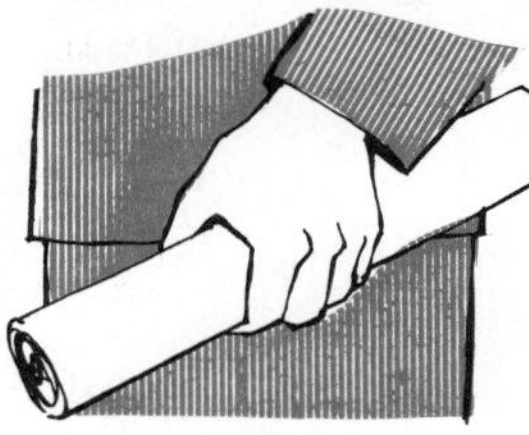

10.

11.

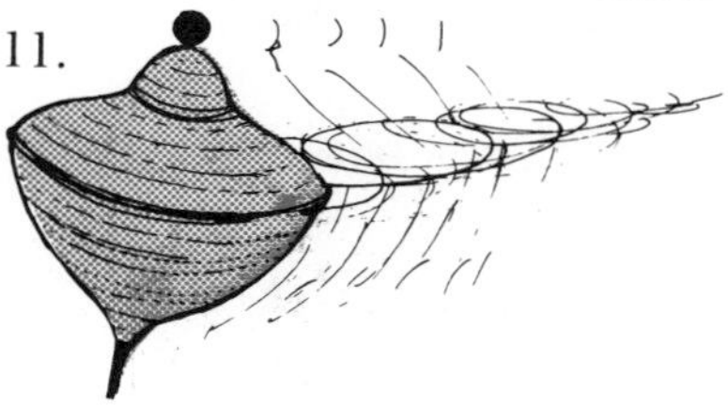

12.

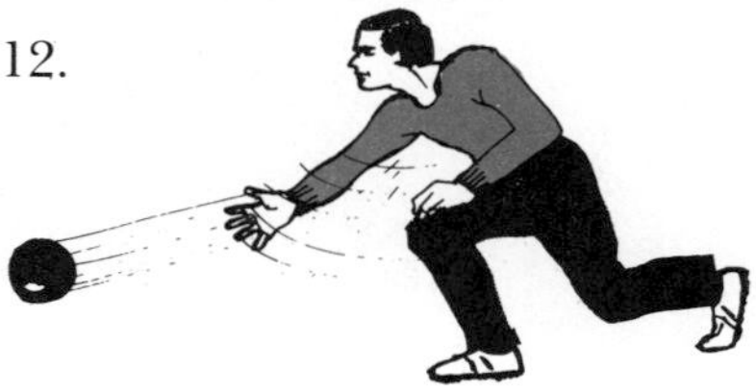

C	N	I	M	U	L	A	F	E	S	L	L	A	W	N	O	T	R	A	C
L	O	U	R	F	C	G	S	O	G	I	V	E	M	R	T	E	H	T	M
A	B	M	P	R	A	P	D	E	X	A	H	O	U	C	H	W	E	T	A
P	E	R	B	O	I	L	R	T	E	L	T	T	O	B	R	K	L	M	I
F	N	A	C	W	R	E	E	B	T	E	K	S	A	B	O	H	N	S	A
R	S	P	I	N	E	S	S	A	C	E	H	C	A	T	W	L	F	Z	A
T	P	L	I	W	C	U	P	K	S	T	H	G	I	N	Y	O	R	V	F
U	Q	B	E	L	C	U	B	I	T	H	G	I	L	D	E	W	A	R	D
R	A	O	B	E	O	K	C	S	J	X	A	W	L	C	R	E	T	R	A
D	C	M	A	R	P	A	S	S	G	H	O	L	D	H	L	A	R	A	P
A	T	N	D	A	S	E	L	G	N	A	I	T	R	O	D	N	I	L	Y
N	E	B	R	E	F	M	U	C	R	I	C	S	U	P	F	T	R	S	C

67 Containers

■ Decide which of the following containers to use.

barrel	**suitcase**	**shopping bag**
sandwich bag	**thermos**	**plastic garden bag**

1. You are going shopping and need a **shopping bag**.
2. You are going on a trip and need a __________.
3. You are packing a lunch and need a __________.
4. You are making coffee for a picnic and need a __________.
5. You are working in the yard and need a __________.

■ ■ Use your *Oxford Picture Dictionary* to help you fill in the following blanks. There may be more than one correct answer.

1. Put **money** in a wallet.
2. Put __________ in a basket.
3. Put __________ in a bottle.
4. Put __________ in a barrel.
5. Put __________ in a paper cup.
6. Put __________ in a carry-on case.
7. Put __________ in a box.
8. Put __________ in a trunk.
9. Put __________ in a crate.
10. Put __________ in a jar.
11. Put __________ in a can.
12. Put __________ in a carton.

68 Lines and Shapes

■ ■ Find as many vocabulary words for *Lines and Shapes* as you can in the following picture. Number them on the picture and write the words below.

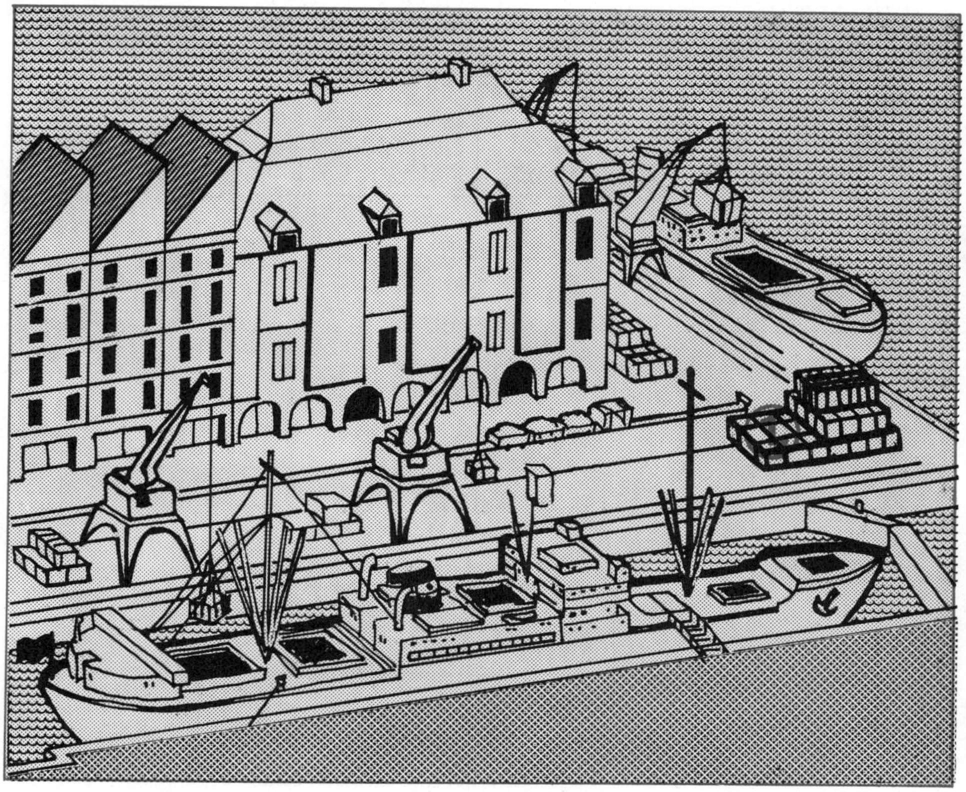

1. cube ____________
2. ____________
3. ____________
4. ____________
5. ____________
6. ____________
7. ____________
8. ____________
9. ____________
10. ____________
11. ____________
12. ____________
13. ____________
14. ____________
15. ____________
16. ____________
17. ____________
18. ____________
19. ____________
20. ____________

68 Lines and Shapes

Find the names of each of these shapes. They are hidden inside each drawing. Some words are backwards and some are diagonal. Write them correctly below each drawing.

1.

I D L O S I H E V R U C T H E

curve

2.

A M T H E S I G E H T N I C P O H A R C I P C L E J F

3.

Z P S T V L
Z I G Z A G

4.

E
S O G
C O N E T
J A W E L B R
C S R T F P U S T

5.

H T S K P U C N L P T
A P A R A L L E L H T
B Z L I N E S Q A D Y
I M L K R B O T T L E

6.

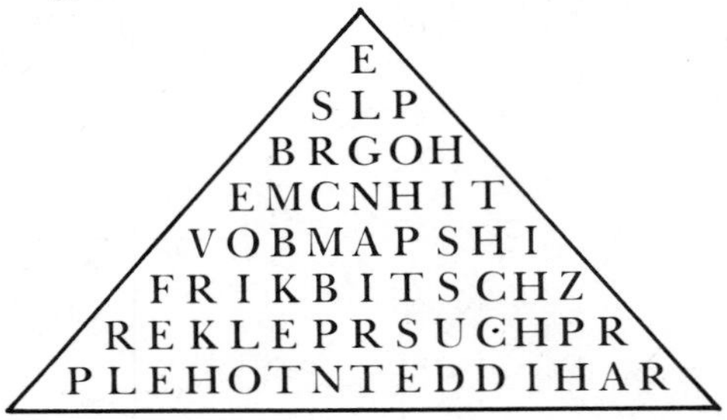
E
S L P
B R G O H
E M C N H I T
V O B M A P S H I
F R I K B I T S C H Z
R E K L E P R S U C H P R
P L E H O T N T E D D I H A R

7.

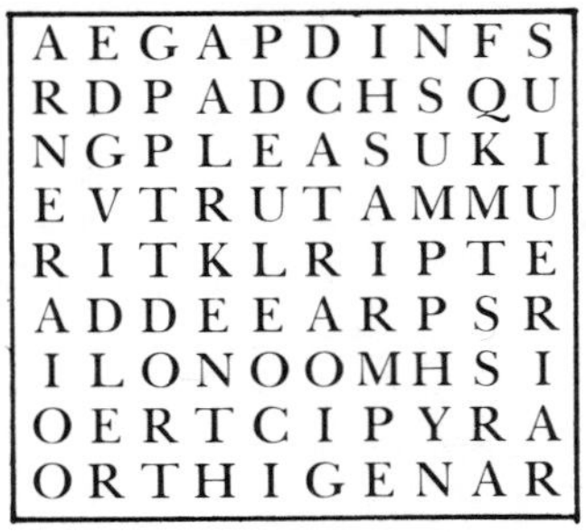
A E G A P D I N F S
R D P A D C H S Q U
N G P L E A S U K I
E V T R U T A M M U
R I T K L R I P T E
A D D E E A R P S R
I L O N O O M H S I
O E R T C I P Y R A
O R T H I G E N A R

8.

C S R T F P U S C I R C U M R
R E C T A N G L E A T E W H C
A R T E T C L W A X J S C K O
M T H E T R M E V I G O S G C

9.

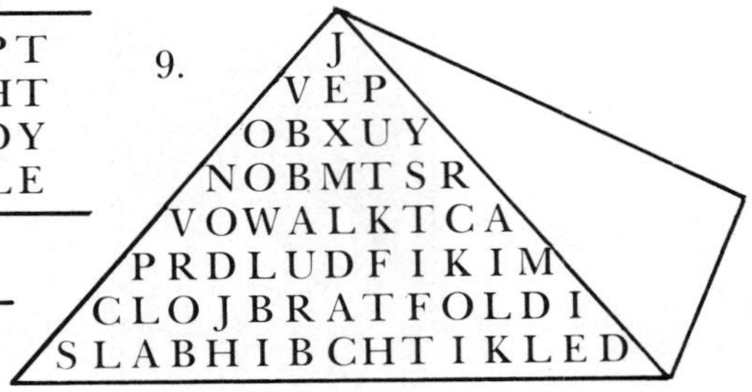
J
V E P
O B X U Y
N O B M T S R
V O W A L K T C A
P R D L U D F I K I M
C L O J B R A T F O L D I
S L A B H I B C H T I K L E D

10.

G A S L I C K
P R I C H U J
E L A D N B F
F R M C D E V

11.

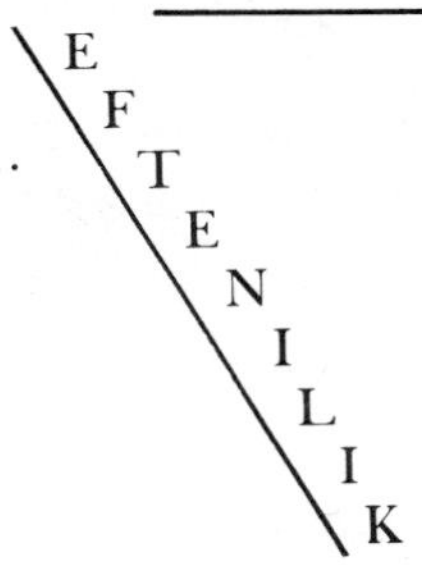
E F T E N I L I K

12.

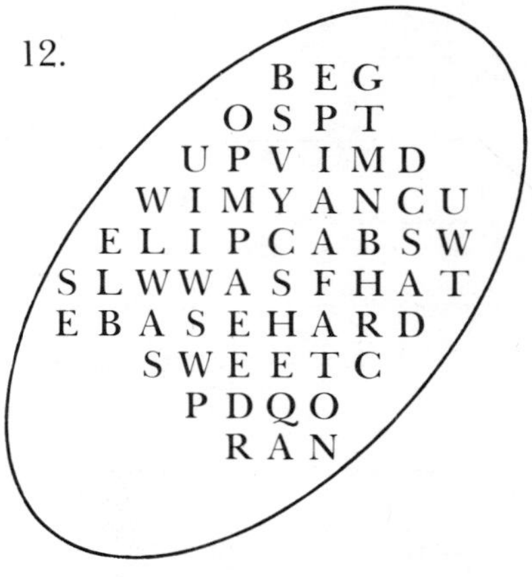
B E G
O S P T
U P V I M D
W I M Y A N C U
E L I P C A B S W
S L W W A S F H A T
E B A S E H A R D
S W E E T C
P D Q O
R A N

69

Measurement

■ ■ ■ Look at the graph and answer the following questions.

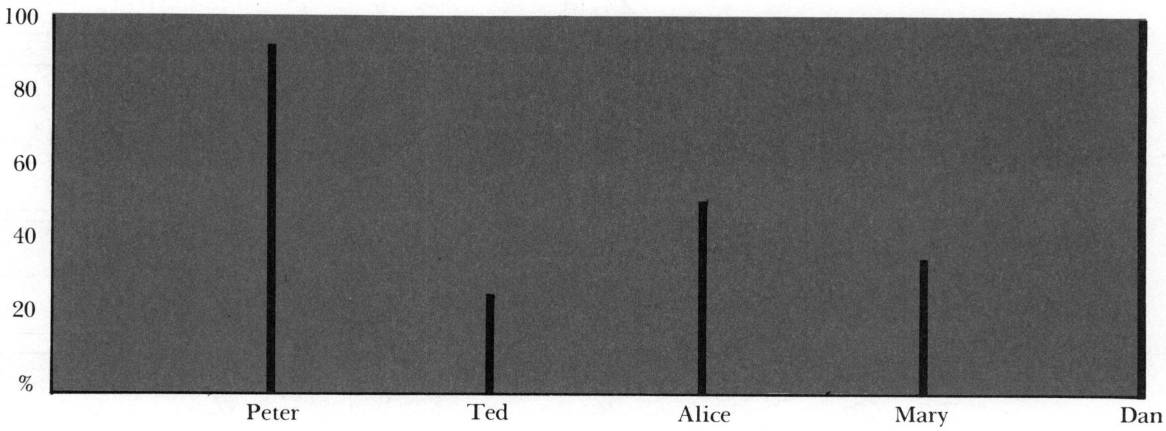
100
80
60
40
20
%
Peter
Ted
Alice
Mary
Dan

1. Which student got 90% of the problems correct? ________________ did.

2. Which student got the best grade? ________________ did.

3. Which student got half of the problems correct? ________________ did.

4. Which student got a quarter of the problems correct? ________________ did.

5. Which student got a third of the problems correct? ________________ did.

■ ■ ■ Write each of these fractions as a decimal, and then as a per cent.

A. a half or .50

or 50%

B. a quarter or ____________

or ____________

C. a third or ____________

or ____________

D. three quarters or ____________

or ____________

■ ■ ■ What fraction of the circle is dark?

E.  ____________

F.  ____________

G.  ____________

H.  ____________

69 Measurement

■ ■ ■ Look at the drawing and answer the following questions.

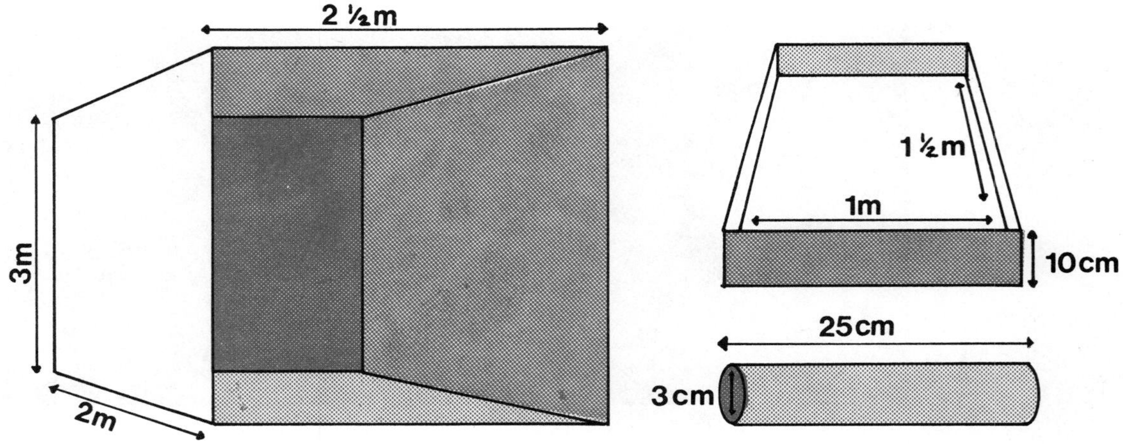

2 ½m
3m
2m
1 ½m
1m
10cm
25cm
3cm

1. What is the height of the box? It is ________________ high.

2. What is the depth of the box? It is ________________ deep.

3. What is the width of the box top? It is ________________ wide.

4. What is the length of the cylinder? It is ________________ long.

5. What is the distance around the bottom of the drawer? It is ________________ around.

6. How long is the side of the drawer? It is ________________ long.

7. What is the length of the side of the drawer minus the length of the front of the drawer? It equals ________________.

8. What is the height of the box plus the depth of the box? It equals ________________.

9. What is the height of the cylinder multiplied by the length of the cylinder? It equals ________________.

10. What is the depth of the box divided by the height of the drawer? It equals ________________.

70 Time, Date, Temperature

■ Give the time and the date for each of the following examples. The *Appendix* at the back of this book will help you. Write out all the numbers as words.

1. 

6/11/45

It was one twenty-five on
June eleventh, nineteen
forty-five.

2. 

3/1/78

3. 

7/9/30

4. 

9/5/48

5. 

4/30/37

6. 

10/4/51

7. 

2/3/09

8. 

11/26/13

9. 

1/2/29

10. 

8/20/52

11. 

12/14/69

12. 

/ /

Today's date and the time.

70 Time, Date, Temperature

■ Some words in English need capital letters and others do not. In each of the following sentences there is **one** mistake. Correct it.

Examples: James will begin school on ~~w~~**W**ednesday.

Today is the ~~F~~**f**irst of April.

1. Where is the Calendar in this room?
2. It is now two-thirty in the Afternoon.
3. What does the Thermometer say?
4. Many people take vacations in august.
5. The Temperature is 65° Fahrenheit.
6. Was January the coldest Month of the year?
7. On Saturday it was only 16° centigrade.
8. In what Year were you born?

■ ■ ■ Answer the questions below in complete sentences. Write out the numbers as words.

1. When were you born?
   I was ______________________________
2. When was the person next to you born?
   ____
3. At what time does your first class begin?
   ____
4. At what time do you leave home for school?
   ____
5. Which is the warmest month in your home country?
   ____
6. How hot does it get during the warmest month?
   ____

71 Family Relationships

■ ■ Fill in the following blanks. Then, put the words into the crossword puzzle below.

ACROSS

1. Carol's sister is Jim's mother.
   Carol is Jim's ____aunt____.

2. Louise is Mrs. Wright's granddaughter.
   Mrs. Wright is Louise's ________________.

3. Mr. Anderson is Tom's father.
   Tom is Mr. Anderson's ________________.

4. Peter and Jane are Mr. and Mrs. Davis's son and daughter.
   Peter is Jane's ________________.

5. Nancy's sister is Betty's mother.
   Betty is Nancy's ________________.

6. Mike's sister is Frank's mother.
   Frank is Mike's ________________.

DOWN

3. Mary and Sam are Mr. and Mrs. Green's daughter and son.
   Mary is Sam's ________________.

7. David's brother is John's father.
   David is John's ________________.

8. Mr. White is Mike's grandfather.
   Mike is Mr. White's ________________.

9. Mrs. Jones is Mary's mother.
   Mary is Mrs. Jones's ________________.

10. Susan and Joe's mothers are sisters.
    Susan is Joe's ________________.

11. Kathy and Robert's parents are Mr. and Mrs. Gibson.
    Kathy and Robert are Mr. and Mrs. Gibson's ________________.

AUNT

73 Nouns of Quantity

■ ■ Use the following words to fill in the blanks in the story below. You will not use all of the words.

box	**tube**	**ball**	**bowl**	**loaf**
piece	**string**	**lump**	**bar**	**cup**
roll	**bottle**	**spool**	**pack**	**glass**

A BUSY DAY

It is Monday morning and Marge Harrison has many things to do today. First, she must bake a cake because it is her husband's birthday. He will get a big ______________ of cake after dinner. The Harrisons are also going to have a ______________ of wine with their dinner. The children will have a ______________ of milk.

Mrs. Harrison must also go shopping today. She needs a ______________ of bread, a new ______________ of toothpaste, a ______________ of blue thread, a ______________ of paper towels, and a ______________ of cookies. At noon, her children will come home for lunch. She will fix a ______________ of soup and a sandwich for each one. About 3:00 in the afternoon, Mrs. Harrison will sit down, put one______________ of sugar in a ______________ of strong coffee and get out her ______________ of cigarettes. She likes to rest and read the newspaper for about half an hour before she starts to prepare dinner.

■ ■ ■ Now that you have read the paragraph, answer the following questions.

1. What day of the week is it? ______________________________
2. Why is Mrs. Harrison going to bake a cake? ______________________________

   ____
3. What does Mrs. Harrison do after she reads the newspaper? ______________

   ____

72 73

Nouns of Quantity

■ Match the words that go together. Then write the phrases in the spaces provided.

1. flowers	o	a. **pack**
2. twine	______	b. **string**
3. cookies	______	c. **crowd**
4. thread	______	d. **swarm**
5. cake	______	e. **bottle**
6. stones	______	f. **flight**
7. beads	______	g. **fleet**
8. people	______	h. **team**
9. paper	______	i. **spool**
10. wine	______	j. **bowl**
11. birds	______	k. **bar**
12. houses	______	l. **pile**
13. bees	______	m. **piece**
14. ships	______	n. **ball**
15. cattle	______	o. **bunch**
16. stairs	______	p. **box**
17. players	______	q. **roll**
18. cigarettes	______	r. **herd**
19. soup	______	s. **row**
20. soap	______	t. **flock**

1. a bunch of flowers
2. ______
3. ______
4. ______
5. ______
6. ______
7. ______
8. ______
9. ______
10. ______
11. ______
12. ______
13. ______
14. ______
15. ______
16. ______
17. ______
18. ______
19. ______
20. ______

74 Adjectives

■ Match the adjectives on the left with their opposites on the right.

1. shallow	__________	a. **little**
2. happy	__________	b. **hard**
3. large	__________	c. **slow**
4. fat	__________	d. **sharp**
5. crooked	__________	e. **dry**
6. easy	__________	f. **cold**
7. blunt	__________	g. **open**
8. soft	__________	h. **sad**
9. fast	__________	i. **thin**
10. wet	__________	j. **dirty**
11. big	__________	k. **low**
12. long	__________	l. **full**
13. hot	__________	m. **difficult**
14. shut	__________	n. **small**
15. high	__________	o. **short**
16. empty	__________	p. **straight**
17. clean	__________	q. **deep**

■ ■ What adjectives would you use to describe the following nouns?

Example: a cup of coffee **hot or cold; full or empty; large or small.**

1. a house ____________________
2. a child ____________________
3. a knife ____________________
4. a street ____________________
5. a dress ____________________
6. a book ____________________

75 Adjectives

■ ■ Read the following advertisement for a house. Some of the adjectives are underlined. Cross out the underlined adjectives and put in the opposite word. Read your advertisement to the class. Does it sound strange?

FOR SALE

UGLY
~~BEAUTIFUL~~ NEW HOUSE

If you are looking for a big house in good condition, you will love this one! The rooms are wide, the wood is solid, and the walls are thick. The floors are all very smooth. You will love the neighborhood too. You'll never hear loud music here! A pretty, neat garden surrounds the house. Be the first people to see this new house. The price is very good! Even a young couple could afford this house!

■ ■ ■ Now describe what *you* think would be the perfect house.

____

____

____

____

____

74 | 75

Adjectives

■ ■ ■ Together with a classmate write a dialog that could take place in a shoe store. Use as many adjectives as possible.

Clerk: ______________________________

Customer: ______________________________

Clerk: ______________________________

Customer: ______________________________

Clerk: ______________________________

Customer: ______________________________

Describe the pair of shoes that you are wearing.

My shoes ______________________________

____

____

____

Describe another article of clothing that you are wearing. For example: shirt, skirt, pants, dress, blouse.

____

____

____

____

76

Prepositions

■ Look at the following prepositions and the picture below. Then, fill in the blanks with the correct preposition. You will not use all of the words.

in front of	**down**	**on**	**into**	**out of**
inside	**against**	**beneath**	**next to**	**behind**
outside	**near**			

9
8
1
6
7
2
3
4
5
10
11

1. Glass **2** is ________________ glass **1**.
2. Glass **3** is ________________ glass **2**.
3. Glass **4** is ________________ glass **5**.
4. Glass **6** is ________________ the top shelf.
5. Glass **7** is ________________ the side of the shelf.
6. Glass **8** is ________________ glass **9**.
7. Glass **9** is ________________ glass **8**.
8. Glass **10** is ________________ glass **11**.

76 77 Prepositions

■ ■ Choose the correct prepositions and fill in the blank spaces below.

Mr. Brown was walking ____________ (to, along, off) the road ____________ (between, on, to) his house ____________ (from, across, beyond) the beach. He saw a friend's dog run ____________ (above, across, at) the road and go ____________ (to, between, off) two cars. It then ran ____________ (along, at, toward) a group of trees and sat ____________ (among, above, on) them. He knew that the dog should not be on the road.

Mr. Brown walked until he was near the dog, but it ran ____________ (off, to, away from) him. Mr. Brown looked ____________ (beyond, above, to) the trees and saw that it was going to rain.

____________ (Along, Between, At) the next corner he saw a policeman and told him about the dog.

Just then Mr. Brown and the policeman saw the dog running ____________ (toward, off, between) the bridge. It was far away. They hoped that the dog would stay ____________ (along, on, off) the road.

■ Match the prepositions on the left with their opposite word on the right.

1. toward	d	**a. on**
2. below	____________	**b. behind**
3. down	____________	**c. to**
4. off	____________	**d. away from**
5. from	____________	**e. inside**
6. into	____________	**f. out of**
7. in front of	____________	**g. up**
8. outside	____________	**h. above**

Appendix

Numbers:

0	zero
1	one
2	two
3	three
4	four
5	five
6	six
7	seven
8	eight
9	nine
10	ten
11	eleven
12	twelve
13	thirteen
14	fourteen
15	fifteen
16	sixteen
17	seventeen
18	eighteen
19	nineteen
20	twenty
21	twenty-one
30	thirty
40	forty
50	fifty
60	sixty
70	seventy
80	eighty
90	ninety
100	a/one hundred
500	five hundred
621	six hundred twenty-one
1,000	a/one thousand
1,000,000	a/one million
1st	first
2nd	second
3rd	third
4th	fourth
5th	fifth
6th	sixth
7th	seventh
8th	eighth
9th	ninth
10th	tenth

Time:

60	seconds (sec.)	= 1	minute (min.)
60	minutes	= 1	hour (hr.)
24	hours	= 1	day
7	days	= 1	week (wk.)
365	days	= 1	year (yr.)
12	months (mo.)	= 1	year
100	years	= 1	century (C.)

Days of the week:

Sunday,	Monday,	Tuesday,	Wednesday,
Sun.	Mon.	Tues.	Wed.
Thursday,	Friday,	Saturday	
Thurs.	Fri.	Sat.	

Months of the year:

January	Jan.
February	Feb.
March	Mar.
April	Apr.
May	
June	
July	
August	Aug.
September	Sept.
October	Oct.
November	Nov.
December	Dec.

January 24, 1956 = 1/24/56
(month) (day) (year)

Appendix

Aa Bb Cc Dd Ee Ff Gg
Hh Ii Jj Kk Ll Mm Nn
Oo Pp Qq Rr Ss Tt Uu
Vv Ww Xx Yy Zz

1 2 3 4 5 6 7 8 9 10

Aa Bb Cc Dd Ee Ff Gg
Hh Ii Jj Kk Ll Mm Nn
Oo Pp Qq Rr Ss Tt Uu
Vv Ww Xx Yy Zz

1 2 3 4 5 6 7 8 9 10

Answer Key

Our Universe — page 3

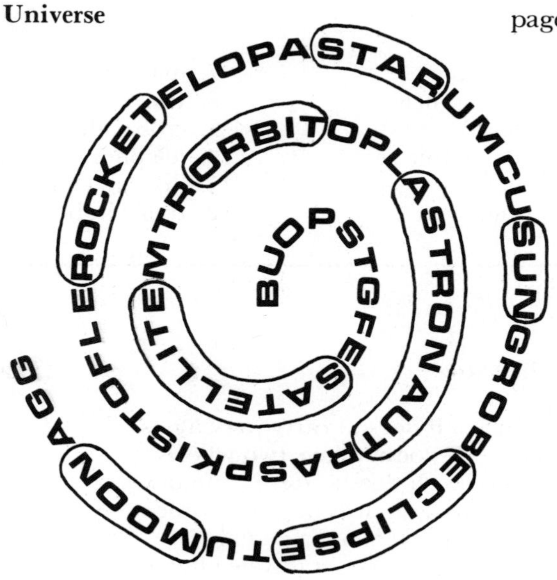

PUZZLE: solar system

Our Universe — page 4

1. full moon	6. earth, a planet
2. A nosecone	7. space capsule
3. An astronaut	8. galaxy
4. stars, a constellation	9. comet
5. a launching pad	10. sun

The World — page 5

1. Ganges   It is not a mountain range.
2. Amazon   It is not a continent.
3. island   It is not water.
4. Danube It is not an ocean.
5. Mekong It is not a desert.
6. Mississippi   It is not in Africa.
7. Caspian Sea   It is not open water.
8. Tropic of Cancer   It is not south of the equator.
9. coastline   It is not imaginary.
10. Arctic   It is not a continent.
11. Persian Gulf   It is not off North America.
12. Australia   It is not attached to other land.

The World — page 6

ACROSS	DOWN
1. Arctic	5. Indus
2. Australia	6. Gulf
3. Robert	7. Sahara
4. Dacca	8. Pole
	9. Bay
	10. Andes

The World — page 7

1. Europe	8. Black
2. Red	9. Africa
3. Gobi	10. Mekong, Yellow, Yangtze
4. Hudson	11. Kalahari
5. Andes	12. Alaska
6. Nile	13. Alps
7. Mediterranean	

The Human Body — page 8

1. A	4. C	7. D or A	10. E
2. C	5. D	8. C	11. C
3. B	6. A	9. A	12. D

1. rib	7. wrist
2. pelvis	8. skull
3. back	9. spine
4. fingernail	10. heel
5. neck	11. throat
6. chest	12. shoulder

The Human Body — page 9

1. mouth	11. chin
2. eyebrow	12. eyelashes
3. cheek	13. mustache
4. pupil	14. iris
5. nose	15. vein
6. heart	16. tongue
7. muscle	17. temple
8. beard	18. lung
9. tooth	19. windpipe
10. brain	20. artery

Clothes: Men and Boys page 10

1. No...bathrobe.
2. No...boots.
3. No...(under) shorts.
4. No...shoes.
5. No...jacket.
6. No...pajamas.
7. No...T-shirt.
8. No...is wearing socks.
9. No...is wearing a belt.
10. No...is not wearing socks.

Clothes: Men and Boys page 11

1. watch
2. overcoat
3. pocket
4. raincoat
5. briefcase
6. sole
7. gloves
8. collar
9. glasses
10. slacks
11. scarf
12. button
13. lapel

briefcase, overcoat, shoelace, watchband, trenchcoat, raincoat

Clothes: Women and Girls page 12

1. G
2. J
3. H
4. A
5. I
6. B
7. C
8. D
9. E
10. F

turtleneck sweater, pantsuit, (shoulder) bag/purse, suit, blouse, handkerchief, coat, dress, kneesocks, sweater, shirt, jeans, sandals

Clothes page 13

UNDERWEAR	NIGHTWEAR	RAIN GEAR
panties	bathrobe	rain hat
panty hose	slippers	trenchcoat
T-shirt	pajamas	rubber boots
shorts	nightgown	umbrella
bra		
slip		

JEWELRY	FOOTWEAR	COSMETICS
cuff links	boots	mascara
bracelet	socks	eye shadow
earrings	slippers	lipstick
necklace	loafers	nail polish
ring	sneakers	
	rubber boots	

In the City page 14

1. bus stop
2. parking meter
3. sidewalk
4. intersection
5. bridge
6. gutter
7. mailbox
8. van
9. crosswalk
10. telephone booth
11. display window
12. traffic light

In the City page 15

1. truck It doesn't carry passengers.
2. van It doesn't have two wheels.
   bicycle It doesn't have a motor.
3. parking lot It is not for people.
4. bus stop It is not a container.
5. sidewalk It is not traveled by cars.
6. mailbox It is not underground.
7. park It is not part of the street.
8. traffic light It is not a sign.
9. baby carriage It doesn't have a motor.
   motorcycle It doesn't have four wheels.
10. trash can It is not a sign.

The Law page 16

policeman, flashlight, uniform, dog, station, car, guard, nightstick, fingerprints, magnifying glass, Gun, judge, jury, witness, stand, defense attorney, cell, bars.

Fire and Medical Services page 17

ACROSS	DOWN
1. drill	1. department
2. dentist	2. doctor
3. patient	3. assistant
4. extinguisher	4. engine
5. bandage	5. nozzle
6. boot	6. nurse
7. hospital	7. crutches
8. smoke	8. hydrant
9. hose	9. ladder

Education: In School

page 18

1. chalk
2. calendar
3. ruler
4. compass
5. map
6. glue
7. protractor
8. slide rule
9. blackboard
10. teacher
11. pen
12. desk
13. pencil
14. student
15. eraser

Education: In the Science Laboratory

page 19

ACROSS

1. scale
2. tripod
3. pestle
4. dial
5. needle

DOWN

1. slide
2. tubing
3. pipette
4. beaker
5. lens

In the Supermarket

page 20

ACROSS

1. fruit
2. vegetables
3. sack
4. eggs
5. freezer
6. milk
7. shelf

DOWN

1. cashier
2. cheese
3. canned
4. bills
5. clerk
6. receipt
7. bread

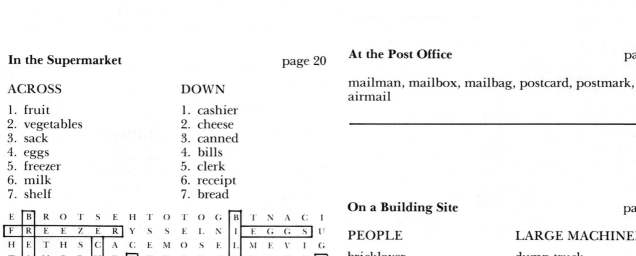

E	B	R	O	T	S	E	H	T	O	T	O	G	B	T	N	A	C	I
F	R	E	E	Z	E	R	Y	S	S	E	L	N	I	E	G	G	S	U
H	E	T	H	S	C	A	C	E	M	O	S	E	L	M	E	V	I	G
T	A	M	O	R	H	F	R	T	X	G	W	A	L	C	I	T	A	C
E	D	D	R	V	E	G	E	T	A	B	L	E	S	I	A	H	H	A
F	T	N	A	C	E	S	C	T	O	R	A	P	M	R	E	C	S	N
O	C	S	A	L	S	E	E	M	I	L	K	W	S	A	Y	A	L	N
G	S	C	K	N	E	A	I	H	T	S	O	O	T	A	K	S	C	E
F	R	L	E	D	N	O	P	W	A	S	I	G	N	I	V	H	I	D
X	R	E	E	Y	F	O	T	E	M	I	T	L	F	R	U	I	T	U
T	E	R	S	S	A	C	K	T	N	I	O	P	T	I	Z	E	A	M
A	C	K	E	B	S	E	L	A	H	W	E	V	A	S	A	R	I	T
C	N	U	R	C	Z	A	G	S	H	E	L	F	E	H	T	E	S	N

In the Office

page 22

ACROSS

1. calculator
2. stapler
3. bookcase
4. blotter
5. typewriter

DOWN

1. calendar
7. steno pad
8. photocopier
9. switchboard
10. file

In the Office

page 23

office, switchboard operator, telephone, receptionist's, appointment, bulletin board, photocopier, secretary, carbon paper, typewriter, envelopes, in-box, adding machine, calculator, desk, blotter, pencil holder, card file, wastepaper basket, file cabinet.

At the Post Office

page 24

mailman, mailbox, mailbag, postcard, postmark, airmail

On a Building Site

page 26

PEOPLE

bricklayer
workman

LARGE MACHINERY

dump truck
excavator
cement mixer

SMALL TOOLS

shovel
trowel
hod
level
pick

PARTS OF A BUILDING

foundations
shingle
rafter

Words not used: scaffolding, wheelbarrow

On a Building Site — page 27

ACROSS

1. board
2. crane
3. cement
4. shingle
5. hod

DOWN

4. sand
6. pick
7. rung
8. rafter
9. trowel
10. brick
11. level

In a Workshop — page 28

1. No
2. No
3. Yes
4. No
5. Yes

1. Yes, it is.
2. No, it isn't.
3. Yes, it is.
4. No, it isn't.
5. Yes, it is.

1. No, it isn't. It's on the shelf.
2. No, it isn't. It's on the wall.
3. No, it isn't. It's on the wall.
4. No, it isn't. It's on the wall.

In a Workshop — page 29

1. nail It doesn't cut.
2. pliers It is not for pounding.
3. vise It doesn't involve paint.
4. nail It doesn't have thread.
5. drill It is not a tool part.
6. shelf It is not for rubbing.
7. plane It doesn't chop.
8. extension cord It doesn't hold things together.
9. hammer It is not a tool part.
10. screwdriver It is not a surface.

A House — page 30

ACROSS

1. curtains
2. shutters
3. windowpane
4. blind
5. patio

DOWN

4. box
6. chimney
7. roof
8. gutter
9. garage
10. door

A House — page 31

house, roof, shutters, walls, balcony, patio, curtains, blinds, garage, shed, grass, window, windowsills, door

---

The Weather/The Yard — page 32

snow, snowman, yard, icicle

rain, flowers, laundry, clothesline

sun, sky, cloud, storm

leaves, tree, branches, twigs, lawn

The Hall — page 33

1. switch
2. telephone book
3. dial
4. receiver
5. stair
6. mail slot
7. hook or rack
8. rug
9. banister
10. floor
11. mat
12. hinge

PUZZLE: welcome

The Living Room — page 34

ACROSS

1. amplifier
2. couch
3. magazine
4. shelf
5. end table

DOWN

1. ashtray
2. ceiling
6. mantel
7. fire

The Kitchen — page 36

sugar bowl
coffee pot
place mat
napkin holder
tea kettle
garbage can

pepper shaker
dish towel
can opener
fruit basket
bread box
frying pan

Household Objects page 37

scrub brush—scouring powder
dust brush—dustpan
washing machine—soap powder
plug—socket
iron—ironing board
mop—pail

1. broom
2. cord
3. switch
4. hair dryer
5. mop
6. pail
7. plug
8. dustpan
9. soap
10. washing machine

The Bedroom/The Baby page 38

BEDCLOTHES

pillowcase
bedspread
blanket
sheet

FURNITURE

stool
desk
crib
night table
chest of drawers
changing table
dressing table
bed

TOYS

rattle
doll
game
stuffed animal

BABY CLOTHES

diaper
sleeper
bib

The Bedroom/The Baby page 39

bedroom, baby, crib, bed, toy, box, rattle, stuffed, pacifier, diaper, powder, bib, bottle

drawers, desk, doll, game, rug

The Bathroom page 40

1. mat
2. tub
3. sink
4. mug
5. glass
6. soap
7. rack
8. tile
9. rod
10. hamper

The Bathroom page 41

bathroom, medicine, razor, glass, bathtubs, mats, water, faucet, shower, curtain

1. washcloth 2. sponge
3. towel 4. scale 5. toothbrush

In the Country page 42

ACROSS

1. hill
2. river
3. pond

DOWN

4. village
5. road
6. wood

In the Country page 43

village, mountains, meadow, river, stream, hills, valleys, lake, waterfall, woods, forests, plateau

road, fields, path, hedge, pond

Camping and at the Seaside page 44

1. kite It is not used in the water.
2. seaweed It is not for camping.
3. rocks They are not to play with.
4. sand castle It is not to stay in.
5. cliff It is not water.
6. boardwalk It is not a person.
7. backpack It is not found on a beach.
8. ice cream It is not to spread out.
9. motorboat It is not used on sand.
10. sunbather He/She is not clothing.

1. A surfer
2. A sunbather
3. A camper
4. A boater
5. A backpacker

On the Farm page 45

1. a barn
2. a hen
3. wheat
4. a calf
5. a hayloft
6. a pen
7. a rooster
8. a field
9. mane
10. An irrigation canal
11. a duckling
12. a barnyard
13. a chick
14. a farm house
15. a furrow
16. a saddle
17. a lamb
18. a bull
19. an orchard
20. a hoof

On the Farm page 46

1. wheat
2. orchard
3. chickens
4. goats
5. rooster
6. pond
7. fence
8. fields
9. tractor
10. scarecrow

Power page 47

ACROSS

1. coal
2. dam
3. reservoir
4. pylons
5. refinery
6. smokestack

DOWN

2. derrick
4. pipeline
7. storage
8. powerhouse
9. cable

Travel by Road page 48

1. taillights
2. turn signal
3. windshield wipers
4. speedometer
5. brakes
6. gearshift
7. ignition
8. radiator
9. battery
10. spark plugs
11. headlights
12. antenna

PUZZLE: repair

Travel by Road page 49

1. wagon
2. accelerator
3. dashboard
4. windshield
5. bumper
6. exhaust
7. engine
8. brake

Travel by Road page 50

1. The transporter is on the overpass.
2. The sports car is in front of the ambulance.
3. There is one car at the gas station.
4. The trailer truck is behind the transporter.
5. The thruway has six lanes.
6. The motorcycle is in the left lane.
7. The sports car is passing the bus.
8. The attendant is in front of the gas pump.
9. The oil truck is in the inside lane.
10. The car is behind the van.

Travel by Road page 51

saddlebag, headlight, gearshift, crossbar, mudguard, footrest, handlebars

1. cable You don't wear a cable.
2. spokes They don't concern light.
3. seat It is not a person.
4. accelerator It is not part of a wheel or tire.
5. taxi It doesn't have two wheels.
6. pump It doesn't concern taxis.

Travel by Train page 52

1. engineer
2. luggage rack
3. engine
4. conductor
5. gate
6. track
7. switch
8. platform
9. flag
10. ties

Travel by Water page 53

ACROSS
1. cable
2. forklift
3. bollard
4. cargo
5. buoy

DOWN
6. horizon
7. wharf
8. pier
9. anchor
10. hold

Travel by Water page 54

1. trawler
2. paddle
3. deck
4. oar
5. mast
6. barge
7. sail
8. ferry
9. bow
10. keel

PUZZLE: the captain

Travel by Air page 55

airport, customs, passport, officer, control, airplanes, runway, hangar, engines, stewards, stewardesses, passengers, luggage, pilot

National Defense page 56

PEOPLE	WEAPONS	VEHICLES
pilot	grenade	bomber
soldier	rifle	jeep
navigator	machine gun	warship
	revolver	tank
	bayonet	submarine
	pistol	fighter plane
		aircraft carrier

Words not used: parachute, cockpit

Recreation: Sport page 57

1. ping-pong
2. wrestling
3. skiing
4. fishing
5. football
6. racing
7. judo
8. hockey
9. tennis
10. baseball
11. table-tennis
12. basketball
13. ice-skating
14. boxing

Recreation: Sport page 58

1. j
2. i
3. g
4. h
5. b
6. a
7. e
8. c
9. d
10. f

Recreation: Sport page 59

1. horse racing A ball is not used.
2. baseball It is not for two people.
3. fisherman He doesn't need snow.
4. net It doesn't concern racing.
5. ice-skating It is not a team sport.
6. scoreboard It is not used to hit with.
7. bat It is not a person.
8. basketball It is not for one person.
9. helmet It is not worn on hands.
10. judo It doesn't involve a ball and net.
11. boxer He is not a football player.
12. jockey He is not a baseball player.
13. boxing It doesn't involve a ball.
14. football It is not a round ball.
15. saddle It is not a place.

Recreation: Music page 60

1. stool
2. strings
3. trombone
4. drum
5. baton
6. trumpet
7. slide
8. clarinet
9. piano
10. mouthpiece

Recreation: Music — page 61

STRINGED INSTRUMENTS

viola
guitar
violin
double bass
cello

PERCUSSION INSTRUMENTS

cymbals
drum

WIND INSTRUMENTS

horn
saxophone
trombone
trumpet

PEOPLE

player
musician
singer
conductor

Words not used: microphone, speaker, music

Recreation: Leisure — page 63

movies, balcony, screen, seats, aisle, movie theater, actress, actor, curtain, usherettes, wings, stage, spotlight, projector

---

Recreation: Bar/Restaurant — page 64

PEOPLE

waiter
bartender
cocktail waitress
customer

CONTAINERS

jigger
can
pepper shaker
ashtray
mug
pepper mill
saltshaker
wine glass
bottle

TOOLS

straw
corkscrew
lighter
bottle opener

LIQUIDS

soft drink
wine
draft beer
hard liquor

Recreation: Bar/Restaurant — page 65

ACROSS

1. stool
2. corkscrew
3. check
4. saltshaker
5. straw

DOWN

1. liquor
2. tap
3. ash
4. menu
5. cocktail

```
C N U R T X O B T E K S A B L E C A B N A C H S A R T
E A W C N O Y R A C E S A C T I O G N I P O H S E T A
A S A L T S H A K E R G A L B N C R A G C I T S A L P
I U S L A P A R W S O M R I E H K U C R E P A P N A C
S N H N E T L L A B T E K Q C A T C H E C K I O F M U
M F T F E L R E T T A B R U I P A R E H S I F T R U O
E L D A S P U R I N A M E O S A I N O C E S R E D T L
N L G N I X O B E T S S T R A W L F E R S R U P H A D
U E L T S E R W E L D I R B S N E D R A O B K C A P B
L O G S T O O L N A G O B O T K A R E T R A U Q O D U
M C O L R A D S S A L D N I W K A S C O R K S C R E W
```

Recreation: Hobbies — page 66

ACROSS

1. spines
2. lens
3. chess
4. photographer
5. diamonds

DOWN

4. pawn
5. deck
6. illustrations
7. hobby
8. projector

Sewing and Knitting — page 67

1. c 3. a 5. d
2. e 4. b

1. ruffle   It doesn't hold clothing together.
2. knitting needle   It is not very sharp.
3. thimble   It is not material.
4. sewing machine   It is not a technique.
5. material   It is not metal.

Occupations/Professions page 68

1. clown
2. carpenter
3. mechanic
4. typist
5. butcher
6. announcer
7. waitress
8. artist
9. porter
10. longshoreman
11. miner
12. dressmaker

Occupations/Professions page 69

ACROSS

1. (An) optician
2. gardeners
3. sailor
4. barber
5. soldiers

DOWN

6. photographer
7. (A) salesman
8. nurse
9. teachers
10. doctor

Occupations/Professions page 70

1. carpenter He has nothing to do with food.
2. miner He has nothing to do with health.
3. typist She doesn't wear a uniform.
4. teacher She doesn't work on buildings.
5. bank teller He doesn't work with plants.
6. redcap He doesn't make or take pictures.
7. dressmaker She doesn't work with vehicles.
8. policeman He doesn't work with hair.
9. clown He doesn't sell things.
10. longshoreman He doesn't work inside.

Occupations/Professions page 71

1. a baker
2. a nurse, doctor
3. a dressmaker
4. a photographer
5. a fruit seller
6. a waitress
7. a policeman
8. an announcer
9. a teacher
10. a mechanic
11. an electrician
12. a carpenter
13. an optician
14. a hairdresser
15. a florist
16. a longshoreman
17. a salesman
18. a typist
19. a butcher
20. an artist

Animals page 72

1. donkey
2. kitten
3. snout
4. whisker
5. camel
6. antler
7. rabbit
8. hump
9. puppy
10. hedgehog

Animals page 73

1. puppy
2. foal
3. flipper
4. reindeer
5. leopard
6. snout
7. whale
8. hump
9. elephant
10. seal

Animals page 74

1. octopus
2. spider
3. centipede
4. eel
5. frog
6. shark
7. snail
8. crab
9. swordfish
10. scales
11. gills
12. scorpion
13. worm
14. salmon
15. lobster

PUZZLE: pearl

Animals page 75

1. He is a biologist.
2. He has a collection of butterflies and moths.
3. They become beautiful butterflies and moths.
4. He wants to find a mantis.
5. Two wasps and a bee stung him.

Animals page 76

1. penguin
2. turkey, goose, pheasant
3. parrot, parakeet
4. swan, ostrich, heron, flamingo, peacock
5. ostrich
6. peacock, pheasant
7. hummingbird
8. flamingo
9. swallow
10. canary
11. peacock, heron
12. crow, blackbird
13. ostrich
14. eagle, hawk, owl
15. vulture

Plants page 77

Ingredients: peach, grapes, pear, strawberries, banana, pineapple, orange, walnuts

Recipe: peaches, bananas, grapes, strawberries, pineapple, pears, orange, walnuts, lemon, orange

Plants page 78

1. plum
2. peanut
3. stone
4. fig
5. cherry
6. core
7. vine
8. grapefruit
9. rind
10. date
11. mango
12. cactus

Plants page 79

1. l
2. g
3. m
4. n or a
5. a or n
6. k
7. c or m
8. f
9. i
10. h
11. j
12. b
13. d
14. e

Plants page 80

1. False
2. True
3. False
4. False
5. True
6. False
7. True
8. True
9. False
10. False
11. True
12. False
13. True
14. True
15. False

Verbs page 81

1. No, he isn't. He's crying.
2. No, they aren't. They're fighting.
3. No, she isn't. She's dreaming.
4. No, he isn't. He's jumping.
5. No, he isn't. He's drowning.
6. No, he isn't. He's climbing.
7. No, she isn't. She's dancing.
8. No, she isn't. She's drinking.
9. No, he isn't. He's drawing.
10. No, she isn't. She's catching a ball.

Verbs page 82

1. She is stirring the coffee.
2. The girl is pulling the cart.
3. The man is shooting the gun.
4. The lady is tying the package.
5. The man is shutting the door.
6. She is sewing the material.
7. He is washing his clothes.
8. The child is reading the book.
9. The man is pushing the door.
10. They are sailing the boat.
11. The woman is tearing the paper.
12. The girl is sweeping the floor.

Verbs page 83

paint, walk, ride, run, sit, listen, swim, sing

Verbs

page 84

1. She is waving her hand.
2. He is turning the wheel.
3. He is beating the drum.
4. He/She is picking the flower.
5. He is winding his watch.
6. She is combing her hair.
7. He is throwing the ball.
8. She is writing a letter.
9. He is ironing his shirt.
10. He is kissing his wife
11. He is passing the truck.
12. He is clapping his hands.
13. He is giving the package.
14. He is holding the paper.
15. He/She is chopping the wood.

Verbs

page 85

C	N	I	M	U	L	A	F	E	S	L	L	A	W	N	O	T	R	A	C
L	O	U	R	F	C	G	S	O	G	I	V	E	M	R	T	E	H	T	M
A	B	M	P	R	A	P	D	E	X	A	H	O	U	C	H	W	E	T	A
P	E	R	B	0	I	L	R	T	E	L	T	T	O	B	R	K	L	M	I
F	N	A	C	W	R	E	E	B	T	E	K	S	A	B	0	H	N	S	A
R	S	P	I	N	E	S	S	A	C	E	H	C	A	T	W	L	F	Z	A
T	P	L	I	W	C	U	P	K	S	T	H	G	I	N	Y	O	R	V	F
U	Q	B	E	L	C	U	B	I	T	H	G	I	L	D	E	W	A	R	D
R	A	O	B	E	O	K	C	S	J	X	A	W	L	C	R	E	T	R	A
D	C	M	A	R	P	A	S	S	G	H	O	L	D	H	L	A	R	A	P
A	T	N	D	A	S	E	L	G	N	A	I	T	R	O	D	N	I	L	Y
N	E	B	R	E	F	M	U	C	R	I	C	S	U	P	F	T	R	S	C

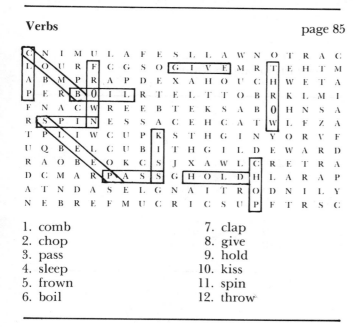

1. comb
2. chop
3. pass
4. sleep
5. frown
6. boil
7. clap
8. give
9. hold
10. kiss
11. spin
12. throw

Containers

page 86

1. shopping bag
2. suitcase
3. sandwich bag
4. thermos
5. plastic garden bag

1. money
2. flowers, eggs
3. milk, juice
4. apples
5. water
6. cosmetics
7. books
8. clothes
9. oranges
10. peanut butter
11. beer, soda
12. dishes

Lines and Shapes

page 87

1. cargo: cube, square, side, right angle
2. roof: zigzag, triangle, apex, base, hypotenuse
3. flag: wavy line
4. warehouse: rectangle, parallel lines, perpendicular line, arc
5. windlass: circle, radius, circumference, diameter, center, section

Lines and Shapes

page 88

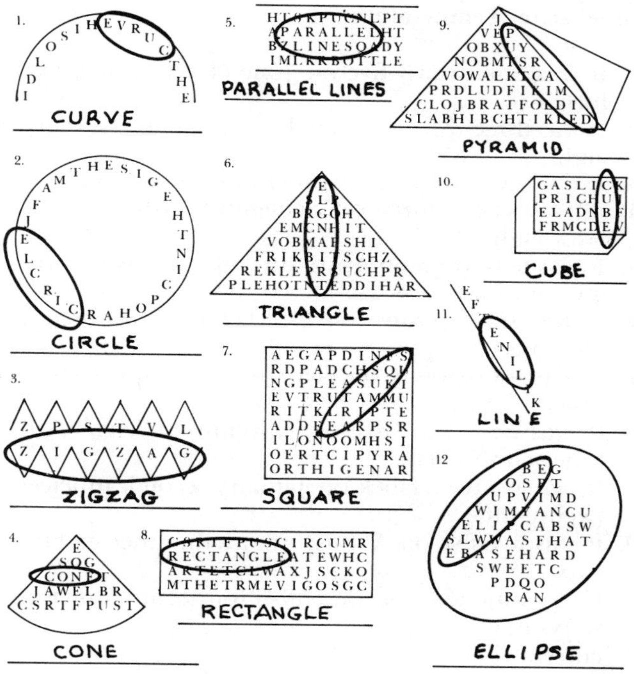
1. CURVE
2. CIRCLE
3. ZIGZAG
4. CONE
5. PARALLEL LINES
6. TRIANGLE
7. SQUARE
8. RECTANGLE
9. PYRAMID
10. CUBE
11. LINE
12 ELLIPSE

Measurement

page 89

1. Peter
2. Dan
3. Alice
4. Ted
5. Mary

A. .50 or 50%
B. .25 or 25%
C. .333 or 33 1/3%
D. .75 or 75%

E. 1/2 F. 1/4 G. 1/3 H. 3/4

Measurement page 90

1. 3 m
2. 2 m
3. 2½ m
4. 25 cm
5. 5 m
6. 1½ m
7. ½ m
8. 5 m
9. 75 cm
10. 20 cm (2 m = 200 cm 200 ÷ 10 = 20 cm)

Time, Date, Temperature page 91

1. It was one twenty-five on June eleventh, nineteen forty-five.
2. It was three-thirty on March first, nineteen seventy-eight.
3. It was seven o'clock on July ninth, nineteen thirty.
4. It was eight-thirty on September fifth, nineteen forty-eight.
5. It was ten-fifteen on April thirtieth, nineteen thirty-seven.
6. It was six forty-five on October fourth, nineteen fifty-one.
7. It was four-twenty on February third, nineteen oh nine.
8. It was two thirty-five on November twenty-sixth, nineteen thirteen.
9. It was twelve o'clock on January second, nineteen twenty-nine.
10. It was five-five on August twentieth, nineteen fifty-two.
11. It was nine-forty on December fourteenth, nineteen sixty-nine.
12. current time and date

Time, Date, Temperature page 92

1. calendar
2. afternoon
3. thermometer
4. August
5. temperature
6. month
7. Centigrade
8. year

Family Relationships page 93

ACROSS

1. aunt
2. grandmother
3. son
4. brother
5. niece
6. nephew

DOWN

3. sister
7. uncle
8. grandson
9. daughter
10. cousin
11. children

Nouns of Quantity page 94

piece, bottle, glass, loaf, tube, spool, roll, box, bowl, lump, cup, pack

1. It is Monday.
2. It's her husband's birthday.
3. She starts to prepare dinner.

Nouns of Quantity page 95

1. o	6. l	11. t	16. f
2. n	7. b	12. s	17. h
3. p	8. c	13. d	18. a
4. i	9. q	14. g	19. j
5. m	10. e	15. r	20. k

Adjectives page 96

1. q
2. h
3. n or a
4. i
5. p
6. m
7. d
8. b
9. c
10. e
11. a or n
12. o
13. f
14. g
15. k
16. l
17. j

Adjectives page 97

beautiful—ugly, new—old, big—little, good—bad, wide—narrow, solid—hollow, thick—thin, smooth—rough, loud—soft, pretty—ugly, neat—sloppy, first—last, new—old, good—bad, young—old

Prepositions page 99

1. beneath
2. near
3. next to
4. on
5. against
6. in front of
7. behind
8. inside

Prepositions page 100

1. along
2. to
3. from
4. across
5. between
6. toward
7. among
8. away from
9. above
10. At
11. toward
12. off

1. d	3. g	5. c	7. b
2. h	4. a	6. f	8. e